The New Songwriter's Guide to

MUSIC
PUBLISHING

3RD EDITION

EVERYTHING YOU NEED TO KNOW
TO MAKE THE BEST PUBLISHING DEALS
FOR YOUR SONGS

RANDY POE

WRITER'S DIGEST BOOKS
www.writersdigest.com

Visit our Web site at www.writersdigest.com for information on more resources for writers.

To receive a free weekly e-mail newsletter delivering tips and updates about writing and about Writer's Digest products, register directly at our Web site at http://newsletters.fwpublications.com.

10 09 08 07 06   5 4 3 2 1

Library of Congress Cataloging-in-Publication Data

Poe, Randy
   The new songwriter's guide to music publishing / by Randy Poe.—3rd ed.
      p.   cm.
   Rev. ed. of: Music publishing. Rev. ed. 1997.
   ISBN 1-58297-383-0 (pbk. : alk. paper)
      1. Popular music—Writing and publishing. I. Poe, Randy.
      Music Publishing. II Title.

MT67.P75 2005
070.5'794—dc22   2005020237
                                                                         CIP

Edited by Amy Schell
Interior designed by Sandy Conopeotis Kent
Cover designed by Claudean Wheeler
Production coordinated by Robin Richie

DEDICATION

For Mina and Riley

ACKNOWLEDGMENTS

I couldn't have written the first, second, or third editions of this book without the input of a number of people. Many thanks go to the following: Robin Ahrold, Connie Ambrosch-Ashton, April Anderson, Ed Arrow, Lew Bachman, Pat Baird, Marilyn Bergman, Jim Bessman, Kevin Bowe, Del Bryant, Steve Day, Roger Deitz, Bob Fead, Arlene Fishbach, Gary Ford, Jane Friedman, Dr. Betty Gipson, Morton Gould, Ellie Greenwich, Julia Groh, Peter Guralnick, Rupert Holmes, Dave Jasen, Ellen Bligh Jones, Jai Josefs, Michael Kerker, Lily Kohn, Bob Leone, Lou Levy, Irv Lichtman, Aaron Lynn, Helen Mallory, Tom McCaffrey, Bob Merlis, Frank Military, Linda Newmark, Norman Odlum, Brendan Okrent, Ralph Peer II, Doc Pomus, Scott Porterfield, Frances W. Preston, Rundi Ream, Pat Rogers, Phyllis R. Rosenberg, Gary Roth, Jeffrey S. Sacharow, Charles J. Sanders, Rick Sanjek, Jerry Schilling, Joan Schulman, Karen Sherry, Alison Smith, Andrew Solt, Greg Sowders, Kathy Spanberger, Al Staehely, Jim Steinblatt, Jane Stevens, Ann Sweeney, William Velez, Cynthia Weil, Bobby Weinstein, George David Weiss, Terry Woodford, and Claudean Wheeler.

Special thanks, as always, to Jerry Leiber and Mike Stoller for the day job. At twenty years and counting, it's still a thrill getting to hang out with my childhood (and adulthood) heroes on an almost daily basis.

Julie Wesling Whaley edited the first and second editions of the book. This time around, Amy Schell handled that duty with a combination of skill, diplomacy, and constant encouragement. I couldn't have done it without her.

Also, thanks to my father and mother, Bill and Marjorie Poe; my sister, Linda Young; my brother-in-law, Gene Yasuda (the real writer in the family); and my mother-in-law, Kayoko Yasuda.

Very special thanks and lots of love to my wife, Mina, and to my son, Riley, for putting up with my many years of late nights in front of the computer.

Finally, I want to thank the late Sammy Cahn. He was, without question, one of the greatest lyricists of the twentieth century. His offer to write the foreword to the first edition of this book back in 1990 helped to give a first-time author's work a real touch of class. I am eternally grateful.

Author Bio

Randy Poe is the president of Leiber & Stoller Music Publishing, a company whose copyrights include such classic hits as "Jailhouse Rock," "Kansas City," "Love Potion #9," "Spanish Harlem," and "Stand By Me." For five years, Poe was Executive Director of the Songwriters Hall of Fame. He is a Grammy-nominated record producer, and author of *Squeeze My Lemon: A Collection of Classic Blues Lyrics.* He lives in Los Angeles with his wife and son.

TABLE OF CONTENTS

FOREWORD

When Randy Poe, who is almost like a son to me, called and asked if I would write a foreword to a book he had written, I was more than happy to oblige. Music publishing is a unique and fascinating part of what words and music are all about. I have vivid and lasting memories of music publishers. For instance, one of the very first music publishers I ever met was a gentleman called Joe Davis. His office was in the Roseland building the famed Roseland of the Dime-a-Dance Ballroom. Joe Davis's office couldn't have been more than two tiny rooms. On the wall there was a sign that I can still see. It simply read, "A contract a day keeps the landlord away." I am sure it did then and I am sure that it does today.

From the Roseland building, I next encountered the DeSylva, Brown & Henderson building on the northeast corner of 49th Street. An amazing number of publishing companies filled this building, and on a hot New York day, before air conditioning, with all the windows open, you could hear the din of all the Tonk pianos going at the same time. (I often wonder if the phrase "Honky-Tonk" comes from the piano of the name?)

As time went on, the publishers moved from the east corner of 49th Street to the now famed Brill Building on the northwest corner of 49th and Broadway. In time came Radio City, and again the publishers moved.

So, now that you know about where they came from, what about them? Well, the publishers I used to know were all the most marvelous and wonderful and colorful people. The songwriters I knew then were (well, most of them) naive and romantic and totally involved with creating words and music totally *un*involved with the business behind the management of their songs. This was "the publisher's domain."

And it was a joyful and rewarding business, especially when you came up with a hit for the publisher. The songwriter then (and maybe now as well) signed whatever contract was placed before him. He was so happy about having a publisher take his song, he didn't stop to think that maybe he was being taken as well.

The early contracts between a writer and his publisher were seemingly rather simple, but they often contained many traps in the small print that benefitted the publisher. It was only after The Songwriters Guild came along that many of the injustices were eliminated.

This book is an absolute guide to avoiding such problems, a guide to the proper procedures for signing a music publishing contract, and for understanding what the terms of that contract should be. Unfortunately, the neophyte writer is seldom in a position to ask for or to dictate any terms. But, assuming the publisher really wants your song, then you are in an enviable position providing you understand the terms you should be asking for. This book explains those terms to you. I really wish there was such a guide book around when I started.

Finally, your first concern should be the writing. But, having written, read this book. You will find it invaluable.

—Sammy Cahn, New York City, May 2, 1990.

INTRODUCTION

You have been pounding the pavement for ages. You've sent CDs of your songs to dozens of music publishers. You've set up appointments with publishers, who have listened to your songs while you fidgeted nervously in an uncomfortable chair.

The CDs that you've sent in the mail have come back either unopened or with brief rejection letters. The publishers you have actually met have all politely turned down your material.

But you have hounded the assistant to the creative manager of a very important music publishing company for weeks. You've called so many times that she has even mentioned your name to her boss.

One day, while the assistant is out to lunch, the creative manager answers your call himself. He almost never makes appointments to listen to material by songwriters he doesn't know. But it's Friday, he's just gotten his paycheck, he's in a great mood, and Monday seems like it's a year away. So he agrees to see you and listen to your songs Monday morning at ten o'clock sharp. Besides, he's sure he's heard your name somewhere. You might be someone he can't afford to ignore.

Having achieved this major victory, you spend the weekend picking exactly which three songs you want him to hear. You're so excited it's almost impossible to sleep Sunday night.

For years you have dreamed of seeing your name in parentheses just below the title of your song on a CD by your favorite artist—or by any artist for that matter. In a few hours you'll be meeting with the person who can help turn that dream into a reality.

At 9:58 on Monday morning you arrive at the publishing company's office and finally meet that assistant you have spoken to a hundred times. She ushers you into the creative manager's office.

He's on the phone, but he smiles and motions for you to have a seat. The chair is extremely comfortable. He's talking and laughing with whomever is on the other end of the line. He is obviously in a very good mood. You're beginning to feel relaxed and at home.

He hangs up the phone, extends his hand, introduces himself as Bob and says, "Let's hear these songs of yours."

You give him your CD. He puts it in his CD player, and your song demo comes floating out through the giant speakers of his two-thousand-dollar sound system. Bob smiles. You smile. For some reason your song sounds better to you than it ever has before—and it's not because of those expensive speakers. The melody flows; the lyrics are almost poetic; and the hook is so good that the assistant sticks her head in the door, smiles at her boss, and gives you an approving nod. By the second verse you can hear Bob tapping his foot to the rhythm. When the hook comes around this time he's actually singing along! Bob listens to the song all the way through to the end. When it's over, he has a look of amazement on his face. The entire scene is repeated as he listens to the second song, and then to the third one. He asks if you have any other songs with you. Of course you do.

As he begins listening to the next CD, you realize that no publisher has ever listened beyond your first three songs before. In fact, at other meetings, most of your time was spent watching the publisher's back as he was hunched over his CD player, skipping from one song to the next, listening only to the first few lines of each song before stopping the CD and handing it back to you with a polite "No thanks."

Suddenly you're back in the present. Bob has just listened to the last song you brought with you. He begins to talk excitedly about an exclusive. You become confused. He's still smiling as he politely explains that a co-publishing deal is possible, but no matter what, he will fight for a strong advance.

You are hearing terms you've never heard before. Bob seems to be speaking in a foreign language. You've never suffered from claustrophobia in your life, but as he begins talking about synchs and mechanicals you start to feel that the walls of Bob's office are closing in around you.

He talks about numbers and percentages; he mentions something about a guy named Harry Fox; and then suddenly he's asking if you're BMI or ASCAP. He seems to really expect you to know what he's talking about.

You're ready to bolt for the nearest door or window. As you're trying to remember what floor you're on, your eyes sweep across the room in search of any exit. On one wall you see a bookshelf. The title of one of the books seems to jump out at you—*The New Songwriter's Guide to Music Publishing*.

Slowly you calm down. The smile returns to your face. You turn back to Bob and say, "I'm really glad that you like my songs and I appreciate the offer you're making. But first I'll need a few days to consider everything we've discussed."

The book you need to read to understand the ins and outs of music publishing is in your hands. All you have to do is turn the page.

PART ONE

The Evolution of the Music Publishing Business

❧ ONE ❧

Music Publishing Yesterday and Today

Music publishing is an industry that is constantly evolving. From the origins of Tin Pan Alley in the late 1800s through the conglomerate craze that exploded in the 1980s and continues to the present day, music publishing has gone through numerous changes for a variety of reasons.

It is conceivable that one could become involved with music publishing today and learn all of the technicalities of the business without knowing or being concerned about its history. However, I believe it's important to learn how the basic principles of music publishing evolved from the need to establish ownership of songs and collect income from them. And how—despite all of the technological changes over the last hundred years or so, as well as major changes in copyright law—the business of music publishing remains what it has always been: the owner-ship, promotion, and administration of songs.

To prevent this from becoming a history textbook, though, rather than go all the way back to the day Johann Gutenberg began toying with the idea of movable type, let's start at the beginning of the modern era of music publishing in America.

Pre-Tin Pan Alley

Like most other successful American enterprises, the music publishing industry in the United States was spawned by entrepreneurship. Before New York City became music publishing's headquarters in the late 1800s, there were small entrepreneurial music publishers all around the country.

These pioneers didn't necessarily make a career just from publishing music. Neither was it necessarily their foremost business activity. In many cases, the early music publisher was simply a person who owned a printing press. In addition to his usual duties of printing books, posters, stationery, and advertisements, the town printer would, on occasion, be asked by a local musician to print copies of sheet music of his latest composition. In his capacity as a music publisher, the printer would sometimes make a deal with the composer regarding the terms by which the composer and the publisher would share royalties on copies sold. These early agreements later evolved into the modern-day song contract.

If the printer was also a stationer (which was often the case), he usually sold copies of the sheet music in his stationery store. The sheet music would also be sold at the local music store if one existed. To reach beyond the city limits, the printer/publisher frequently hired traveling salesmen to sell the sheet music throughout a particular region on a commission basis. Along with the clothes and household supplies the salesman usually carried on his rounds, he now included a case of sheet music samples as an important part of his product line.

When the traveling salesman came to town, he would sell clothes to the local clothing stores, household supplies to the general store or notions shop, and sheet music to the town's music store and/or the local five-and-dime. The more talented of these salesmen would actually play and sing the songs they had in their sample cases to convince the proprietor of a store to order copies of the sheet music. This early concept of promoting songs later became an extremely important part of the music publishing business.

Among these salesmen were a few who felt there was a growing future in music publishing. These early entrepreneurs—familiar by now with what music was most popular in a particular region—established their own publishing companies. Some wrote and published their own songs. Some acquired new songs from the songwriters whose sheet music they had previously sold on behalf of other publishers. Others began looking for new songwriters to sign to publishing agreements.

Next, it was only a matter of paying a printer to print their sheet music—or, for the braver of this new breed, of acquiring printing presses to make the entire operation an in-house affair. At this point, America was just a beat away from Tin Pan Alley.

Tin Pan Alley

A combination of several events brought about the creation of Tin Pan Alley in New York City during the late 1800s, the foremost of which was improved and cheaper transportation.

By the middle of 1869, America's first transcontinental railway route had been completed. Over the next two decades, tens of thousands of miles of railroad tracks were laid in place. With access to most of the country's major cities now easily available, groups of entertainers originating from New York City traveled all across the country performing their acts in theaters and music halls.

These entertainers were singers, dancers, comedians, jugglers, acrobats, and other types of performers. This traveling variety show was a form of entertainment called vaudeville. Among the show-business legends that were part of the vaudeville world were the Marx Brothers, Fred Astaire, W.C. Fields, and the Four Cohans. (The Four Cohans were a family of performers that included a boy named George. George M. Cohan would go on to write many Tin Pan Alley classics, including "Yankee Doodle Dandy," "Over There," and "Give My Regards to Broadway.") Thanks to vaudeville, music publishers had a constant source of performers in need of new material to take on the road.

In New York City, the theaters, booking agents, and the *New York Clipper* (the industry trade paper of the day) were located around Twenty-Eighth Street. Since this was the area where the entertainers of the era were hanging out, and since those entertainers frequently traveled around

Tin Pan Alley (West Twenty-Eighth Street) at the turn of the twentieth century: the industry trade paper, the New York Clipper; music publisher Jerome H. Remick & Company; and the William Morris Agency. (Photo courtesy of ASCAP archives.)

the country performing songs before large audiences of prospective sheet music buyers, it made good sense for the music publishers to be based in this neighborhood.

Near the end of the nineteenth century, everything seemed to fall into place on and around Twenty-Eighth Street—the area of New York known as Tin Pan Alley. Among the important music publishing companies that made up Tin Pan Alley at the time were M. Witmark & Sons; F.A. Mills; Leo. Feist, Inc.; Harry Von Tilzer Music Publishing Company; and Jerome H. Remick & Company. Several of these firms were created by the salesmen-turned-publishers mentioned earlier.

The general setup of these music publishing companies in the Tin Pan Alley days was relatively simple. The company had an office with one or more rooms, and each room contained a piano. The publisher would hire songwriters to sit in each room during the day and create new songs.

How Tin Pan Alley Got Its Name

As the story goes, a *New York Herald* reporter named Monroe Rosenfeld was assigned to write about the new music publishing industry that had settled in Manhattan. To gather information for his story, Rosenfeld went to the Harry Von Tilzer Music Publishing Company in the heart of the publishing district. As he exited the building, Rosenfeld heard the many pianos being played at all of the publishing firms along Twenty-Eighth Street. Since this was before the days of air conditioners, windows were open all along the block. In some of the offices there were composers banging out new melodies, while in other offices the composer and lyricist together were demonstrating a new song to a vaudeville performer looking for new material. Rosenfeld later reported that the resultant sound on the street was similar to that of tin pans banging against each other. Although Monroe Rosenfeld didn't actually use the phrase "tin pan alley" in his *New York Herald* piece, he did refer to Twenty-Eighth Street between Sixth Avenue and Broadway as "the Alley" and, as a result, Tin Pan Alley became the new name of the area where music publishing houses were clustered together in New York City.

Competition among the publishers was fierce. New songs were needed constantly. Up and down Twenty-Eighth Street, composers banged out new melodies while lyricists stood by, trying to come up with catchy phrases to fit their partners' tunes. Once the Tin Pan Alley songwriter or songwriting team had finished a new song, it was the publisher's job to go out and persuade an entertainer to add the number to his act. This process, which originated with the Tin Pan Alley publishing companies, became known as *song plugging*.

An example of the lengths some song pluggers would go to involves legendary music publisher Lou Levy. In 1936, Levy was managing the young songwriting team of Sammy Cahn and Saul Chaplin, who had written a song called "Shoe Shine Boy." "The building at 729 Seventh Avenue was filled with talent agencies and music companies," Levy recalled. "I gave the elevator operator fifty cents a day to sing 'Shoe Shine Boy' as he went up and down in the car. His passengers would ask him about it and he'd say, 'Oh, that song is gonna be a big hit. You ought to get onto it right away.'"

For many of the publishers who had begun as salesmen, it seemed only natural that once the product was created, every effort should be made to see that it was sold. Since song plugging was a new concept, there were no ground rules. Whether the plugger was the publisher himself or a hired hand capable of singing, playing, or whistling a tune, the only rule was to go out and persuade someone—the more well-known the better—to perform the song the song plugger was plugging.

After an entertainer agreed to perform the number, the publisher would print sheet music of the song—often with a picture of the performer on the cover. (The performer's picture was included to appeal to the entertainer's ego and to encourage the performer to keep the number in his act.) The sheet music would then be distributed to wholesalers (or *jobbers*) throughout the country in preparation for the orders that would, hopefully, begin pouring in from the retailers.

The performer—along with his fellow vaudeville acts—would then go on the road via the now elaborate passenger train system, singing the song at the music halls and theaters of the vaudeville circuit into which he had been booked. (Bookings were usually handled by agencies that were located, like the music publishers, on or near Twenty-Eighth Street.)

Frequently, the day after the popular singer had performed in a particular town, the local music store (and other stores of the day that carried sheet music) would be flooded with requests for copies of the new song that had been sung the night before. And just in case prospective purchasers of the sheet music couldn't remember the song's exact title, they had only to look for the sheet with the picture of the song's performer right there on the cover.

Because pianos had become one of the main sources of entertainment in the home during the 1800s, sheet music was much in demand. In fact, during the vaudeville era, it was the number of copies of sheet music sold that determined whether or not a song was a hit.

The creation and success of Tin Pan Alley, then, can be traced to several factors: the improved railway system; the creation and popularity of vaudeville; the popularity of pianos as a major source of entertainment in the American home; the proximity of the various facets of the entertainment industry in New York City; and the new concepts of how music publishing companies should operate, as devised by the men and women who made Tin Pan Alley run. (These new concepts were: to hire songwriters to create new songs in the popular style of the moment; to plug—or promote—the songs by persuading performers to add the numbers to their acts; and to market the songs in sheet music form that frequently featured the performer on the cover.)

The result of all of these factors was a remarkable leap in sheet music sales and, consequently, an equally remarkable leap in profits for the music publishers. By the end of the first decade of the twentieth century, millions of copies of sheet music had been sold. Some of the most popular songs of the decade are purported to have sold as many as a million copies *each*.

The Arrival of Recordings, Radios, and Films With Sound

In the early twentieth century, new technology had a profound effect on music publishing. At first, the effect was potentially devastating because the U.S. Copyright Act, on which the principles of publishing are based, failed to keep up with the country's rapid technological growth.

Prior to the U.S. Copyright Act of 1909, there was much confusion about what monies might be owed to publishers by manufacturers of piano rolls. After the law was enacted, the publisher received two cents for each of his songs that appeared on a piano roll or recording manufactured by these rapidly expanding American industries.

Beginning in the 1920s, both recordings and radio had become important new forms of home entertainment, and many vaudeville performers quickly became radio stars. Publishers believed if they could get the stars of this new medium to perform their songs on the radio, sheet music sales were bound to skyrocket. If these stars also made recordings of the songs, then additional profits would be made from record sales.

Before the 1920s were over, another major technological advance arrived that caused substantial changes in Tin Pan Alley. This latest breakthrough was the addition of sound to film. On October 6, 1927, the first movie musical opened. *The Jazz Singer* had been a Broadway hit in 1925; the movie version, starring Al Jolson, was the first film to combine songs with moving images on the big screen. *The Jazz Singer* was a box office smash, prompting Hollywood to turn to Broadway and vice versa.

Former stars of vaudeville and Broadway were soon on their way to California, along with the songwriters who were now in demand by the Hollywood studios. In need of older songs as well as new ones, motion picture companies such as Warner Bros. began to purchase entire publishing companies from their original owners.

Sound recordings became prominent after World War II, and sheet music became a less important part of the music publishing industry. In fact, by the early 1950s, many publishers had begun to "job out" the print portion of their operations to companies who specialized in printing sheet music, song folios, and band, orchestra, and choral arrangements for many different copyright-owning publishers.

This practice has led to today's "print publishers," who sometimes own few or no copyrights of their own. Their business is simply to print and distribute music on behalf of the copyright-holding publishers, who share in the income earned from print sales. Today, very few music publishers still have their own print divisions. The print business—although still important—is now a much smaller aspect of the overall music publishing industry. It's no longer profitable for any but the wealthiest of publishing companies to maintain an in-house print operation.

Elvis Presley and the Birth of Rock and Roll

With the advent of television came the variety show. In 1956, when Elvis Presley appeared on the *Dorsey Brothers Show*, the *Milton Berle Show*, the *Steve Allen Show*, and, finally, the *Ed Sullivan Show*, he not only drove millions of American teenagers wild—he also put panic in the hearts of the older music publishers. In a few brief television appearances, Elvis showed America that popular music had a new name, a new audience, and a new attitude. (Simultaneously, he proved that television—for better or for worse—would become the ultimate entertainment medium of the second half of the twentieth century.)

From this point on, the music publishing industry would either cater to a youthful audience; rest on its laurels and wait for this "latest phenomenon" to blow over; turn its emphasis toward Broadway shows; or head off to Hollywood to be a part of the last few years of the post-golden age of big-budget movie musicals.

Those who chose to wait out the fad are either still waiting, or eventually took an "if you can't beat 'em, join 'em" attitude. Those who took the last train to Hollywood must have been shocked when Elvis and other teen idols rode into town too, taking over the once-sacred Hollywood

Songwriting team Mike Stoller (left) and Jerry Leiber (right) with Elvis Presley. In the early rock and roll era (pre-Beatles), recording artists rarely wrote their own material. They relied on songwriters and music publishers for a steady supply of hit songs. (Photo courtesy of Leiber & Stoller.)

musical. This new Hollywood musical emphasized scores by songwriting teams such as Jerry Leiber and Mike Stoller, Doc Pomus and Mort Shuman, and others who—along with these writers—had helped to create rock and roll. On occasion, older songwriters capable of adapting to this new style of music would compose for the new Hollywood musical as well.

Adaptability, in fact, quickly became a most essential quality in the music industry. New York was still filled with music publishers, including many new ones who specialized in rock and roll. But the writers who had been such an important part of Tin Pan Alley were now either writing almost solely for Broadway and films or had been replaced by teenagers and young adults whose songs were saying what young audiences wanted to hear. Very few songwriters of Tin Pan Alley's heyday were able (or willing) to make the transition to rock and roll.

By the early 1960s, the music publishing industry had caught on to the youthful crazes that were sweeping the country. If Chubby Checker turned young people on to "The Twist," publishers responded with new songs about the popular dance, or at least with new songs that could be twisted to. Meanwhile, Hollywood was quick to base entire movies—mostly low-budget—on the dance craze of the moment.

Many publishers wisely moved into the recording industry, signing acts to record the songs written by the publishing division's staff writers. These independent record/publishing companies now had the best of both worlds. Everything seemed to be working out well for the American music publishing industry until yet another act appeared on the *Ed Sullivan Show*.

Ralph S. Peer

One of the legendary names in music publishing is Ralph S. Peer. In 1920, Peer began his career with OKeh Records where he assisted in the early recordings of numerous black artists including Mamie Smith's "Crazy Blues," a breakthrough million-seller. In 1927, he joined the Victor label as a field-recording engineer and record company A&R man. In August of that year, he went to Bristol, Tennessee, where he held auditions for local artists in the area looking for a chance to make records. Over the course of two weeks in Bristol, among those he auditioned and recorded were Jimmie Rodgers and the Carter Family—two acts that would become among the most important recording artists in the history of country music.

As significant as his discovering Rodgers and the Carters was, equally important was his ability to foresee the potential of copyright ownership of their original songs. Up to this point in time, country music was a niche market virtually ignored by Tin Pan Alley. With that in mind, Peer came up with a plan to create a niche publishing company.

In a brilliant stroke of music publishing entrepreneurship, Peer worked out an arrangement with Victor Records whereby he would draw no salary, but in return would be allowed to control the publishing rights to any original songs written and recorded by artists he was responsible for getting signed to the label.

So, in January of 1928, Ralph Peer formed Southern Music (known today as peermusic), soon acquiring such now-classic songs as "Georgia on My Mind," "Will the Circle be Unbroken," and "You are My Sunshine."

Having had success with both country and blues recordings, Victor decided to seek out artists in the Latin-American market. Ralph Peer was at the forefront of the Latin music movement of the 1930s and '40s, acquiring the publishing rights to Latin-American hits such as "Besame Mucho," "Brasil," and "Perfidia."

Peer was always able to change with the times, signing early rock and roll songwriter/recording artist Buddy Holly, among others, in the late 1950s.

Ralph S. Peer passed away in 1960, but peermusic—which today is the largest independent music publishing company in the world—continues to grow under the leadership of Peer's son, Ralph Peer II.

Seventy-three years after Peer discovered Jimmie Rodgers and the Carter Family in Bristol, Tennessee, the motion picture *"O Brother, Where Art Thou?"* was released. The movie included a half-dozen songs from the peermusic catalog, while its corresponding soundtrack album sold over seven million copies—the ultimate proof that Ralph S. Peer was literally right on the money when he foresaw the vast potential of copyright ownership.

Enter the Beatles

On February 9, 1964, the Beatles took the country by storm when they appeared on Ed Sullivan's Sunday-night variety show, sparking what the press would soon dub the British Invasion. In addition to their unique sound, haircuts, and clothing, the Beatles brought along something American publishers weren't yet prepared to deal with: their own self-penned songs. Suddenly, the world of popular music seemed to be filled with acts that supplied their own material. After all the adapting they had done over the past decade, how were publishers supposed to cope with this new wrinkle? (At least Elvis Presley still needed writers!)

At first the solution was simple. Many publishers were able to convince these self-contained acts that it was still necessary to sign over 100 percent of what is commonly known as the *publisher's share* of their songs to an "established" publisher who could properly promote and administer the compositions. (The concept of publisher's share/songwriter's share is explained in chapter six.)

Rupert Holmes is a singer/songwriter/record producer and Broadway writer/composer/lyricist whose show, *The Mystery of Edwin Drood*, won five Tony awards. His hits as a recording artist include the million-selling, number-one single "Escape" ("The Piña Colada Song"). Holmes says that publishers suddenly became very interested in him as soon as he signed a recording contract with a major label:

> *A transition had taken place in the music industry, which was that publishers were finding that they no longer knew how to get songs recorded because there were not a lot of artists recording outside material—certainly not a lot of artists recording the kind of traditional pop songs that people would sit down and write in the Brill Building.**
>
> *The publishers said, "How are we going to get songs recorded when artists are recording their own songs?" So they decided, "We'll turn it inside out. We won't place the songs. We'll sign the artists who have recording contracts and get their publishing. That guarantees us ten songs on every album they make."*

When Rupert Holmes became a recording artist, he received a very large advance from a major publisher "with a stipulation that {he} would record ten songs every year. It was their way of placing ten songs on an album—just the opposite of how publishers had been doing business for decades."

Because of such industry practices, many well-known acts of the era signed away the publisher's share to publishers who needed to do little more than sit back and watch the money roll in from the record companies and other sources. Before long, many of the self-contained acts (whether they were solo singer/songwriters or bands whose members wrote the material they recorded) began to realize the importance of publishing. With the help of entertainment attor-

---

*The Brill Building, 1619 Broadway in New York City, was once filled with publishers of Broadway shows and traditional pop songs—publishers of the old Tin Pan Alley variety (many of whom had moved up from Twenty-Eighth Street in the post-vaudeville years). During the late 1950s and early 1960s, more modern publishers and several independent record companies moved in. At that time, the Brill Building became the place where such writers as Jerry Leiber, Mike Stoller, Neil Diamond, Doc Pomus, Mort Shuman, Ellie Greenwich, and Jeff Barry created many of their pop classics. Contrary to popular belief, however, the Brill Building was *not* the spot where Carole King, Gerry Goffin, Neil Sedaka, Howie Greenfield, Barry Mann, and Cynthia Weil wrote some of their biggest hits. Their publisher, Aldon Music, was actually in a building across the street and up the block at 1650 Broadway.

neys and better-informed managers, it soon became commonplace for a self-contained act to set up an in-house publishing company. These in-house publishing companies managed the songs written and recorded by the band or singer/songwriter so that, when records were sold, the record company paid publishing royalties to the company owned by the self-contained act, rather than to an outside publisher.

Of course, the record company executives weren't fools. They were aware that many of the jobs that once rested on the publisher's shoulders had now become the record company's responsibility. In the Tin Pan Alley days, when sheet music was the tangible product preferred by the public, it was the publishing company's job to print, distribute, and promote that product. After World War II, when recordings took over as the preferred form of musical entertainment in the home, it became the record company's responsibility to manufacture, distribute, and promote.

Based on this turn of events, in many cases (especially prior to the 1980s), if a self-contained act wanted to sign a recording contract with a particular label, frequently the act also had to sign a publishing agreement with the label's own in-house publishing company. It was in this manner that many record companies became owners of important publishing catalogs containing some of the most valuable rock and roll songs of the 1950s, 1960s, and 1970s. Although similar deals continue to be made today, they are much less common. In fact, on those rare occasions when a label demands that publishing be incorporated into a recording contract, it is usually for only a percentage of the publishing (as opposed to all of it).

Music Publishing Today

There is still a thriving music publishing industry in New York City. California's publishing community has continued to grow as well. But the remnants of Tin Pan Alley—that is, publishers who have staff songwriters and who take their songs to artists daily in an attempt to get their songs recorded—have, for the most part, moved south. Music Row in Nashville, Tennessee, is the current home of the Tin Pan Alley type of publisher. In fact, there is now an annual songwriters' event in Nashville called Tin Pan South. For songwriters who specialize in country songs, Nashville is the place to be—just as Twenty-Eighth Street in New York City was once the place to be for the pop songwriter. There are other publishing and recording centers: Seattle; Minneapolis; Chicago; Memphis; New Orleans; Philadelphia; Boston; Muscle Shoals, Alabama; Austin, Texas; Athens, Georgia; and Jackson, Mississippi have all become centers of various kinds of American music. There are, in fact, many regions throughout the country where publishers can be found.

For the nonperforming songwriter there continue to be many nonsongwriting performers who constantly need new songs. This is something songwriters and publishers everywhere are aware of and are actively pursuing—especially in Nashville. However, to say that a talented nonperforming songwriter has exactly the same chance of success as an equally talented singer/songwriter might not be as accurate a statement as the nonperforming writer would wish.

Today's music publishers have a new attitude about the role they play in the music industry. In many cases, the emphasis has begun to lean more and more toward development deals.

Rather than simply sign a songwriter and hope that he will create something the publisher can convince someone else to record, many publishers now look for that singer/songwriter or self-contained band that the publisher can take into the studio. What the music publisher hopes to come away with is a high-quality demo (or even a finished master recording) that can then be shopped around to the major record labels. In exchange for footing the bill for the demo production costs, the publisher ends up with some portion of the publishing rights to the songs written by the act.

By becoming involved in producing self-contained acts, many music publishers have continued to be flexible enough to remain an active part of the industry, even though the music business has gone through numerous changes over the decades.

BUYING AND SELLING

In recent years, some music publishers have begun to take advantage of a couple of other options: buying in and selling out.

At one time, the music publishing industry was made up of many major companies (each of which owned several thousand copyrights), as well as hundreds of smaller independent companies (each of which owned anywhere from one to several hundred copyrights). As I mentioned earlier, when the Hollywood movie industry began to use songs in films, many of the motion picture companies bought up music publishers as a simple way of acquiring a large number of ready-to-perform songs.

Since that time, the number of publishing companies has grown and shrunk like an accordion. While new companies are constantly being formed, new and old companies alike are also being bought and incorporated into larger companies. In the last two decades, there has been an unprecedented amount of buying, selling, and merging among music publishers.

Perhaps the most publicized of these various acquisitions was Michael Jackson's purchase of ATV Music Publishing for $48 million in 1985. (ATV's catalog includes over 250 songs written by the Beatles.) After purchasing ATV, Jackson turned over the administration of this valuable company to CBS Songs.

Realizing the increased value of CBS, music industry veterans Charles Koppelman and Martin Bandier, along with New York–based financier Stephen Swid, purchased all of the copyrights owned by CBS (as well as the administration rights to those songs being administered by the company) in 1986 at a reported cost of $125 million, forming a publishing company called SBK Entertainment World.

The following year, Warner Communications bought the publishing firm of Chappell & Co. for approximately $250 million, merging Warner Bros. Music and Chappell & Co. into a company called Warner/Chappell Music.

In 1989, CBS Broadcasting—now owned by Sony—got back into music publishing (remember, they had previously sold their publishing division to Koppelman, Bandier, and Swid) by purchasing Tree International, a Nashville-based publishing company, for around $40 million. Initially, this new company was called Sony-Tree, but was later changed to simply Sony Music Publishing.

A few days after CBS acquired Tree, SBK Entertainment World was purchased by Thorn EMI for just over $300 million.

For those who thought Koppelman and his partners were making a mistake when they paid more than a $100 million for CBS's publishing division in 1986, a little math will show that the trio had the proper profit-making philosophy all along: Buy high, sell higher.

But the story doesn't end there. In 1995, a decade after his purchase of ATV, Michael Jackson merged ATV Music Publishing with Sony Music Publishing, creating (at least for a while) the third largest publishing company in the world.

At that time, along with Sony/ATV, BMG, EMI, and Warner/Chappell, there were two other major music publishing companies: MCA and PolyGram. In 1998, MCA's parent company purchased PolyGram, merging the two companies the following year into an entity called Universal Music Group. In 2000, Universal purchased Rondor Music International—one of the largest independent music publishing companies in the world—resulting in Universal having over a million songs in its catalog.

The big question regarding all of these sales, buyouts, acquisitions, and mergers is what happens to all of those songs and songwriters caught up in these transactions. For example, let's say you wrote a song that was signed to a publishing company, only to discover that the company you've signed to is being sold to a giant company tomorrow, and that *that* company is being bought by a huge conglomerate next week. What are the chances of your song receiving proper attention from that huge conglomerate, which will have literally a million other songs to oversee? This is the reality of music publishing today.

Rupert Holmes expresses his view on merger mania:

> *When you're working for a public corporation and you're accountable not only to bosses but also to stockholders, you feel you have to make moves that you can defend on paper. In other words, it isn't so stupid to buy the catalog of a famous songwriter who is now dead. It's a wise investment because it's not that speculative. It's a sound move. The trouble is that sound moves generally: (1) are unexciting; (2) don't change anything in the world; and, (3) often end up being exactly that—sound and boring. That's why I equate a lot of publishers with investment bankers.*

Kevin Bowe is a songwriter/record producer with an extremely impressive track record. His songs have been recorded by dozens of artists—from Jonny Lang to Etta James to Lynyrd Skynyrd—and have appeared on numerous gold and platinum albums totaling over 12,000,000 units sold to date. He also teaches songwriting and music publishing at the McNally Smith College of Music in St. Paul, Minnesota. Like many other songwriters, Kevin takes a dim view of music publishing mergers:

> *I think the insatiable focus on mergers has had a negative effect on the music business. The bottom line in music publishing is that you have to have at least one person at the company who can tell tin from gold—not an accountant, not a trend watcher, not an MBA, not a marketing person—but one person that can tell what people will like—tomorrow. Not the*

day after tomorrow (that person is a visionary and just might bankrupt the company!), not yesterday (that person is already employed as the head of a major record label), but what people will like tomorrow. The corporate culture fostered by these mergers discourages the kind of entrepreneurial thinking that is at the very heart of the marriage of art and business. Not only is there no room left for the development of new writers at these mega companies, there is also no room for the people who can "pick one out of a crowd." These merger-minded companies are in the "futures" business; making their money by forecasting which existing catalogs are worth buying and selling, and when. Any new talent that they sign will be based on what sales that writer has already accomplished, not any potential they see based on the actual quality of the writer's work. In many ways, the music publishing business has moved from Tin Pan Alley to Wall Street.

And what about a songwriter who is signed to a major music publishing company with hundreds of thousands of songs in its catalog? "You're a speck in the cosmos," says Rupert Holmes:

> *There's no way that they can be aware of you. They're not going to call you up at three in the morning with a bright idea about how they can get your song placed.*
>
> *If 80 percent of the world's publishing is owned by a couple of companies, how are they going to be really excited about you? How can they go to a stockholders' meeting and explain about this incredible new songwriter they found in Brooklyn who shows a lot of promise and has found a way to rhyme "orange"? It's not going to be on their list of priorities.*

In the end, a great song is a great song. It will be up to you (whether you're a performing songwriter or not) to write that great song, to learn what the music business is all about, to make the proper contacts along the way, and to be in the right place at the right time. You will also have to be extremely lucky.

In this chapter we have covered over a century of music publishing in America. Yesterday the industry was supported by sheet music. Today the sources of income for music publishers are numerous and diverse. Throughout the intervening decades, copyright laws and technological improvements have changed dramatically, but the function of music publishing has remained constant: the ownership, promotion, and administration of songs.

PART TWO

Music Publishing and Copyright Law

✯ TWO ✯

The Evolution of the Copyright

Understanding what music publishing is first requires an understanding of what copyright is all about. The terms *copyright* and *music publishing* go hand in hand. They don't mean the same thing, but each requires the other in the context of our discussion.

Like a hot dog and a hot dog bun, they are two separate entities, both of which can be "digested" separately. When you put the two together, however, they can be better appreciated.

Definitions of Copyright and Publication

Taken at face value, copyright means (as the Copyright Office aptly explains) "the right to copy." In other words, when you create an original work (such as a song), you own exclusive rights to that work and copies of that work. The reason you acquired those rights is because of the existence of the U.S. Copyright Act.

Publication, on the other hand, is defined by the copyright law as "the distribution of copies or phonorecords of a work to the public by sale or other transfer of ownership, or by rental, lease, or lending" (a phonorecord is basically a sound recording). A published work can also be a work for which there has been an "offering to distribute copies or phonorecords to a group of persons for purposes of further distribution, public performance, or public display."

What the copyright law is saying is that publication doesn't necessarily take effect even when copies are actually printed or pressed. There must also be distribution of copies or an "offering to distribute copies" before something is considered to be published.

A Little Copyright History

The concept of copyright is based primarily on logic. If you create something original, you should be protected from unauthorized copying of your original work. Long before there were copyright laws, there was a commandment that made the same point: Thou shalt not steal.

Copyright laws were devised not only as a form of protection against theft, but also as an inducement for a country's citizens to *create* copyrightable works. If there were no protection and compensation (or the possibility of compensation) for writing songs, books, or plays—or for creating other types of copyrightable material—creative people would be forced to earn their livings in other ways. Of course, many would continue to create original works in any event, but it is unquestionable that the volume of creative works would be greatly reduced without the incentive that copyright laws provide.

In the United States before 1788, Congress didn't have the power to constitute a federal copyright act. When Noah Webster wanted to prevent others from copying his latest work, *American Spelling Book*, he campaigned for copyright legislation in this country.

In response to his efforts, on May 2, 1783, Congress made a recommendation to the thirteen states that they should each create legislation that would protect authors and publishers of books. (As you can see, even

> Once in the public domain, the book, chart, or map became public property and could be reprinted without anyone having to account to the former copyright owner.

at the beginning of copyright history in this country, copyrights and publishing were linked together.) By 1787, twelve of the states had copyright laws in place. All twelve states used a British law dating from 1710—the Statute of [Queen] Anne—as their basic guide.

In 1788 the U.S. Constitution was ratified, giving Congress the power, in the Constitution's words, "To promote the Progress of Science and useful Arts, by securing for limited Times to Authors and Inventors the exclusive Right to their respective Writings and Discoveries." Congress quickly went to work and created the U.S. Copyright Act of 1790, once again patterning the law after the Statute of Anne—a statute that was extremely limited and filled with restrictions and registration requirements. This first federal copyright law gave protection to books, charts, and maps created by U.S. citizens and residents. (Apparently, popular songs—and other types of music—were not yet considered "useful Arts" by Congress. However, some early music publishers were savvy enough to begin putting musical selections in collections and selling them in book form—thus receiving copyright protection under the 1790 law.)

To be guaranteed copyright protection under the 1790 law, one had to record the work's title, before it was published, at the clerk's office of the local district court; have a copy of this fact printed in at least one newspaper for four weeks; and send a copy of the actual book, chart, or map to the Secretary of State's office any time during the first six months after publication. As you can see, government red tape is nothing new.

Since the Constitution said that the copyright should be in effect "for limited Times," the 1790 copyright law stated that an author's work would be protected for fourteen years, with the right to one renewal term of an additional fourteen years. The purpose of putting a limit on the duration of a copyright is to preclude the failure "to promote the Progress of . . . useful Arts." The idea behind this portion of Article I of the Constitution was to prevent a permanent monopoly on a copyright. Thus, under the 1790 law, once the original term of copyright neared expiration, it was necessary to renew the copyright by going through the business with the clerk's office and the newspaper again.

If these steps for proper renewal weren't taken, the once-copyrighted work fell into the public domain. Once in the public domain, the book, chart, or map became public property and could be reprinted without anyone having to account to the former copyright owner. Needless to say, allowing a copyright to go PD before the end of its full twenty-eight year life span was the ultimate faux pas among copyright owners.

Even if properly renewed, twenty-eight years was as long as a copyright could last at that time. If a book's copyright went into effect in 1800, the book entered the public domain by 1829, no matter what. If the author was twenty years old in the initial copyright year, she lost all rights to her own creation by the time she was forty-nine.

Included in a number of revisions to the copyright law in 1831 was the extension of the first term of copyright to twenty-eight years, with the renewal term remaining at fourteen. Luckily for songwriters, the 1831 revisions also included the addition of musical works, allowing songs the potential to be protected for a total of forty-two years.

The loss of a copyright during the copyright creator's lifetime has been a major problem throughout the history of U.S. copyright law. If you began writing songs after December 31, 1977, it is a problem you're not likely to face. However, thousands of copyright owners whose works were in the first term of copyright prior to 1978 fall into a unique category that will require more detailed explanation. (See "Length of Copyright Protection" on page 31).

> Learning about copyright and the music publishing industry is like studying a foreign language—you must develop a new vocabulary.

In 1897, Congress added public performance rights to copyright law. Although several more years would pass before all of the wrinkles were ironed out, the copyright owner now had the right to be paid for public performances of the copyrighted work. Royalties for the public performance of a copyrighted musical work would later become one of the most important sources of income for composers, lyricists, and music publishers.

The Copyright Act of 1909 was a major overhaul of the previous copyright statutes. In one big, all-encompassing act, all of the provisions for copyright protection were laid. One new provision was that the period for the copyright renewal term was now twenty-eight years, making the potential life of a song copyright fifty-six years.

As I mentioned in chapter one, the 1909 act required that a two-cent royalty be paid on copyrighted songs that were reproduced mechanically. At that time, the law was referring to piano rolls and early disc and cylinder recordings. As technology progressed, the law was applied to other forms of mechanical reproduction, such as electrical transcriptions and audiotapes. By 1955, technology and new art forms were making the 1909 act seem quite antiquated, so the Copyright Office—with funding from Congress—began studies in preparation for a major revision of the 1909 law. Working out the many details of a copyright act suitable for the second half of the twentieth century proved to be a difficult task. There were many people whose livelihoods might be improved by a new copyright law, while other people might have to pay out higher royalties or royalties not previously required. After extensive lobbying by all sides, the new copyright law was enacted on October 19, 1976, essentially becoming effective on January 1, 1978.

This new copyright law changed the duration of a copyright, in most cases, to the life of the author plus fifty years for works created after December 31, 1977. There were several other substantial changes from the 1909 law, many of which are still in effect today. Why aren't *all* of the changes still in effect today? One reason is because of something called the Berne Convention Implementation Act of 1988, which allowed the United States to become part of the world's most significant international copyright treaty. President Ronald Reagan signed the Berne Act on October 31, 1988, with the law becoming effective on March 1, 1989. The Berne Act changed only some portions of the 1976 Copyright Act, much of which remains intact.

As it turns out, there have been many changes in copyright law since the implementation of the Berne Act in 1989, so some of the information is no longer accurate (as you will see in the section on p. 31, "Length of Copyright Protection"). One of the things you should keep in mind is that copyright law is not static. In recent years there have been numerous additions to the 1976 law, including the Sonny Bono Copyright Term Extension Act, the Fairness in Music Licensing Act of 1998, and the Digital Millennium Copyright Act. Despite the fact that ongoing changes in the copyright law require songwriters and publishers (and authors of books on the subject of music publishing) to keep abreast of the latest revisions in the law, there is a huge upside. Without the copyright law's continuous updating, we might still be living under the Statute of Anne.

Copyright—Some General Thoughts

Now that you're familiar with some areas of copyright law from a historical standpoint, it's time to get into the specifics of the law currently in effect. Two of the topics most songwriters seem to be concerned about are registration of copyrights and copyright infringement. Both subjects are important and both will be covered in this book, but of equal importance is a general knowledge of what copyright protection is and what it means to you as a copyright owner.

If you haven't already learned about copyright law from a reliable source, you might discover a few surprises here. For instance, you may have heard that you have to fill out a form and send it to the Copyright Office for your song to be copyrighted. Or, you might have been told that it's okay to copy a certain number of notes or measures from another song without being guilty of copyright infringement. These are just a couple of copyright myths that we'll dispose of in the following pages.

One of the main things you're about to discover is that you can't really understand copyright law without learning there are several terms and phrases specifically used in discussions about copyright with which you might not already be familiar. Learning about copyright and the music publishing industry is like studying a foreign language—you must develop a new vocabulary. Just as in learning a foreign language, there are lots of words in the music publishing business that must become a part of your vocabulary.

I learned to speak "music business" over the course of many years and am now at a point where I can hold my own in a roomful of record company executives, musicians, entertainment lawyers, and accountants. It's not unlike my early days of playing around on the Internet: Before

I began to learn the terminology, I didn't know what my Web-obsessed friends were talking about. Once I entered cyberspace myself, I was forced to learn "cyberspeak." Soon I could converse with my friends on their level.

The point is, to be able to communicate knowledgeably with music publishers and entertainment lawyers, you need to be able to speak and understand their language. Once you learn the terminology, you may find yourself more fluent than some people already in the music publishing business—a very enviable position for any songwriter.

THREE

The Six Exclusive Rights of the Copyright Holder

With several notable limitations, the U.S. Copyright Act gives the copyright owner "the exclusive right to do and to authorize others to do" six specific activities.

1. **The right "to reproduce the copyrighted work in copies or phonorecords."** Here we come across the word *phonorecords* again. The definition provided by the 1976 Copyright Act says that phonorecords are:

> . . . *material objects in which sounds, other than those accompanying a motion picture or other audiovisual work, are fixed by any method now known or later developed, and from which the sounds can be perceived, reproduced, or otherwise communicated, either directly or with the aid of a machine or device. The term "phonorecords" includes the material object in which the sounds are first fixed.*

A phonorecord, then, can be a prerecorded audiotape, a record of any speed (remember those?), a compact disc, or any other type of recording that falls into the category of the definition, whether "now known or later developed." When this definition was devised, commercial sales of compact discs didn't exist. Luckily for copyright owners, the definition of phonorecords in the 1976 Copyright Act provided for such future inventions so that revisions in the law wouldn't be required with each new technological development.

Now that we know what phonorecords are, let's get back to the first exclusive right listed above: a copyright owner has the right to "reproduce the copyrighted work in copies or phonorecords," (or to authorize others to do so). Once you have written a song, you have the exclusive right to reproduce copies of that song. If you want to print sheet music of your song, the law says that's one of your rights. Conversely, if someone else wants to reproduce copies of your song, they can do so only if you authorize them to, or if they fall into the category of those exempt from this provision of the copyright law.

(So who's exempt, and why? Earlier, when I said the copyright law gives you some exclusive rights, I prefaced the sentence with the phrase "with several notable limitations." Sometimes copyright law seems a lot like English grammar—for every rule, there seems to be at least one exception. Rather than dwell on the exceptions now, I'll discuss all of them together later in the chapter.)

Allowing the *initial* reproduction of your copyrighted work on phonorecords is an exclusive right that has no limitations. However, once that initial recording has been distributed, the law says anyone can record your copyrighted work as long as a notice of intention is given to you and proper royalties are paid. (As you will recall, the 1909 Copyright Act called for a mechanical royalty of two cents per unit. This provision was updated in the 1976 law. See the discussion of the compulsory mechanical license later in this chapter.)

2. The right "to prepare derivative works based upon the copyrighted work." Here we are again with another term that doesn't come up in everyday conversation: *derivative work*. According to the 1976 Copyright Act definition, a derivative work is:

> *. . . a work based upon one or more pre-existing works, such as a translation, musical arrangement, dramatization, fictionalization, motion picture version, sound recording, art reproduction, abridgment, condensation, or any other form in which a work may be recast, transformed, or adapted. A work consisting of editorial revisions, annotations, elaborations or other modifications, which, as a whole, represent an original work of authorship, is a "derivative work."*

A derivative work, then, can be a number of different things. One example would be the addition of lyrics to an instrumental work that has already gone into the public domain. For instance, if you added lyrics to Beethoven's Fifth Symphony, the result would be copyrightable by you under the definition of derivative work. Of course, since Beethoven's compositions are in the public domain, other people who wished to could also add their own lyrics to that melody without requiring your permission. Theirs would simply be another derivative work—derived from the same music. The fact that your derivative work is copyrightable doesn't mean that Beethoven's Fifth Symphony suddenly wouldn't be in the public domain anymore. Only the derivative work that you created (the combination of your lyrics and his music) would be copyrightable.

To change the situation slightly, let's say you have created an original instrumental piece. Let's say that it became a big hit due to its use in a popular movie. If you allowed someone to add lyrics to your instrumental hit, the result would be a derivative work that would be copyrightable. Of course, in this situation, you would have to come to an agreement with the lyricist as to how royalties would be shared in this new derivative work, since your original copyright would still be alive and well.

On the other hand, if someone adds lyrics to your instrumental piece without your permission, the result is an unauthorized derivative work—an infringement of your copyright. Why? Because the law says you, the copyright owner, have the exclusive right to prepare—or authorize others to prepare—a derivative work. If someone has created an unauthorized derivative work based on your copyrighted material, you have the right to enter into that time-honored music industry tradition of suing the unauthorized party.

One type of derivative work prevalent today is the result of a recording artist "sampling" a pre-existing recording of a song to such an extent that the new work created by the sampler is merely a derivative of the original. (For a thorough explanation of sampling, see chapter four.) For example, let's say I wrote and recorded a song called "Mary Had a Miniature Infant Sheep." Then let's say that another recording artist sampled a large section of my song, added a rap lyric to it, and left my original chorus in. In fact, her version is so derivative of my song, she even wants to call her song "Yo! Mary Had a Miniature Infant Sheep." Assuming I am willing to allow the new lyrics to be added, as the copyright owner of the original work, I could claim "Yo! Mary Had a Miniature Infant Sheep" as a derivative of my copyrighted song. It would be my decision, then, whether to allow the other recording artist to share in the writing credits or the publishing income from her recording of the song.

3. The right "to distribute copies or phonorecords of the copyrighted work to the public by sale or other transfer of ownership, or by rental, lease, or lending." You already know you have the exclusive right to reproduce copies (such as sheet music or recordings) of your copyrighted work. Here, the law goes on to say that another of your rights is to distribute those copies for sale to the public (or to authorize others to do so). As I mentioned in chapter one, today there are print publishers who specialize in the printing, distribution, and selling of sheet music, folios, and other printed versions of a musical composition. However, they can only print, distribute, and sell copies if the owner of the copyrighted work has authorized them to.

The same rule applies to the distribution of phonorecords except that (as I mentioned earlier), after the initial recording has been made, others may distribute new recordings of the song as long as a notice of intention has been given to the copyright owner and as long as the royalties required by law are properly paid.

If you refer to the definition of *publication* at the beginning of this chapter, you will see that this third exclusive right is actually your right to publish your work (or to authorize others to publish it).

4. The right, "in the case of literary, musical, dramatic, and choreographic works, panto-mimes, and motion pictures and other audiovisual works, to perform the copyrighted work publicly." The performance right is one of the most valuable rights a songwriter has. Basically, this right guarantees that (with the exceptions granted by copyright law) no one has the right to perform your song in public except you or those you authorize.

Of course, once you've written a song, it's likely you'll want it to be performed in public as often as possible. Also, although it is possible to stop the unlawful copying or distribution of your song (and thereby prevent the loss of royalties), it would be a pretty difficult task to keep track of all the singers who might be performing your work at any given moment.

To help copyright holders monitor public performances of their work and collect royalties on these performances, there are now three performing rights societies in the United States: AS-CAP, BMI, and SESAC. Their function is to charge licensing fees to a variety of sources that use publicly performed music, including radio stations, television stations, concert halls, night-clubs, and Web sites. Most of the money received by the performing rights societies is then paid to songwriters and publishers. How much money is due to which songwriter and publisher is determined by the various monitoring systems and payment plans that have been devised by the performing rights societies. (All three societies will be discussed in detail in chapter four.)

5. The right, "in the case of literary, musical, dramatic, and choreographic works, pantomimes, and pictorial, graphic, or sculptural works, including the individual images of a motion picture or other audiovisual work, to display the copyrighted work publicly." Of the six exclusive rights of the copyright owner, the right to display ranks as one of the least important to songwriters and music publishers. The exclusive right to display is of extreme importance to the copyright owners of photographs, artwork, motion pictures, and other copyrightable materials that more readily lend themselves to exhibition. But unlike these visual forms of art (or well-behaved children), songs are usually heard, but not seen. Therefore, it's relatively rare that a song would fall into the category of being displayable.

However, when a song appears in sheet music form, the relevance of displayability to the songwriter becomes apparent. If the sponsor of a print advertisement wishes to use a piece of sheet music as a part of her ad, permission to do so would have to be requested of the copyright owner. Occasionally a book about popular music may display a piece of sheet music on the book's cover or as part of the text. This type of use would also require permission from the copyright owner.

In karaoke, the words to a popular song are displayed on a video screen while a prerecorded instrumental track is being played. Under this portion of the copyright law, permission of the copyright owner is required for the lyrics to be displayed.

6. The right, "in the case of sound recordings, to perform the copyrighted work publicly by means of a digital audio transmission." This sixth exclusive right doesn't actually apply to songwriters or music publishers. It was added to the copyright law's list of exclusive rights because of something called the Digital Performance Right in Sound Recordings Act of 1995. The DPRA was created so that record labels (or other copyright owners of sound recordings) can collect performance royalties for certain digital audio transmissions.

Limitations of Exclusive Rights

The law giveth and the law taketh away. As soon as the Copyright Act finishes outlining the copyright owner's six exclusive rights, it then takes several pages to explain all of the limitations of those rights.

The first limitation covered in the act is a concept called *fair use*. The fair use exception applies to all six exclusive rights and grants to anyone the right to reproduce a copyrighted work "for purposes such as criticism, comment, news reporting, teaching (including multiple copies for classroom use), scholarship, or research. . . ." Provided that the use of a copyrighted work falls into the fair use category, that particular use is not considered to be an infringement of the copyright.

The Copyright Act goes on to say that there are four factors to consider in determining what is a fair use. These are:

1. the purpose and character of the use, including whether such use is of a commercial nature or is for nonprofit educational purposes;
2. the nature of the copyrighted work;
3. the amount and substantiality of the portion used in relation to the copyrighted work as a whole;

4. the effect of the use upon the potential market for or value of the copyrighted work.

Since it would be impossible to cover every conceivable variation of what a fair use might be, the law is saying that these are the four guidelines that would be considered if a copyright owner questioned whether a particular use of the owner's work qualified as fair use.

LIMITATIONS ON THE RIGHT TO REPRODUCE COPIES

Under the fair use guidelines provided by the Copyright Act, there are clearly exceptions to the copyright owner's first exclusive right, which is "to reproduce the copyrighted work in copies or phonorecords." The limitations include the right of libraries and archives to make phonorecords in specific situations. Music educators may also make recordings of student performances for study and for school archives.

The other major limitation on the owner's exclusive right to reproduce phonorecords falls in the category of compulsory mechanical licenses. (See the section on the compulsory mechanical license on page 27.)

LIMITATIONS ON PREPARING DERIVATIVE WORKS

Limitations regarding the second right—the right to "prepare derivative works based upon the copyrighted work"—are not specifically covered by the Copyright Act except in its brief section on fair use, which limits all six exclusive rights. However, it is generally agreed that printed copies that have been purchased can be edited or simplified for educational purposes as long as the fundamental character of the work isn't distorted and the lyrics aren't changed.

LIMITATIONS ON THE RIGHT TO DISTRIBUTE COPIES

In reference to the third exclusive right—to *distribute* copies or phonorecords of the copyrighted work—there are no limitations, except for those provided under fair use guidelines and by the compulsory license requirement regarding recordings of a song after the initial recording has been released.

LIMITATIONS ON THE RIGHT TO PERFORM OR DISPLAY

The Copyright Act lists several limitations on the fourth and fifth rights—the rights to perform or display the copyrighted work publicly. Under the law, the following types of performances and displays of a copyrighted work do not require the permission of the copyright holder or the payment of royalties.

1. Performance or display of a work by instructors or pupils in the course of face-to-face teaching activities of a nonprofit educational institution.
2. Performance or display as part of mediated instructional activities transmitted via digital networks.
3. Performance of a nondramatic literary or musical work or of a dramatic musical work of a religious nature, or display of a work, in the course of services at a place of worship or other religious assembly.
4. Performance of a nondramatic literary or musical work otherwise than in a transmission

to the public, without any purpose of direct or indirect commercial advantage and without payment of any fee or other compensation for the performance to any of its performers, promoters, or organizers.

5. Communication of a transmission embodying a performance or display of a work by the public reception of the transmission on a single receiving apparatus of a kind commonly used in private homes.

6. Performance of a nondramatic musical work by a governmental body or a nonprofit agricultural or horticultural organization.

7. Performance of a nondramatic musical work by a vending establishment open to the public at large without any direct or indirect admission charge, where the sole purpose of the performance is to promote the retail sale of copies or phonorecords of the work.

8. Performance of a nondramatic literary work, by or in the course of a transmission specifically designed for and primarily directed to blind or other handicapped persons who are unable to read normal printed material as a result of their handicap, or deaf or other handicapped persons who are unable to hear the aural signals accompanying a transmission of visual signals.

9. Performance on a single occasion of a dramatic literary work published at least ten years before the date of the performance, by or in the course of a transmission specifically designed for and primarily directed to blind or other handicapped persons who are unable to read normal printed material as a result of their handicap.

10. Performance of a nondramatic literary or musical work in the course of a social function which is organized and promoted by a nonprofit veterans' organization or a nonprofit fraternal organization to which the general public is not invited.

It should be noted that the ten limitations listed above have been extremely condensed from the actual wording used in the Copyright Act. The bottom line is that the logic behind these limitations is pretty apparent. Using the first limitation as an example, it would be unrealistic to expect educational institutions to be required to get permission from (and pay royalties to) the copyright owner every time a teacher wants to show students a copyrighted map, or every time a group of first-graders want to perform a copyrighted song in class.

Other Limitations on Copyright

The Copyright Act goes on to list limitations on exclusive rights as they pertain to sound recordings performed by means of digital audio transmissions; ephemeral recordings; secondary transmissions; reproductions of pictorial, graphic, and sculptural works; and on and on. Rather than get bogged down in seemingly endless limitations, let's move on to an area that is of utmost importance to both songwriters and music publishers.

There has been one instance of fair use that the U.S. Supreme Court chose to clarify (sort of) in 1994. When 2 Live Crew recorded a parody version of the song "Oh, Pretty Woman," the publisher of the original song filed an infringement suit. The court ultimately determined that 2 Live Crew's work wasn't copyright infringement because—according to the Supreme Court—it fell under the category of fair use.

As a music publisher with important copyrights to protect, I personally think the decision was unfortunate. In reading the fair use section of the copyright law, it is difficult to see how one could determine that 2 Live Crew's song qualified as such. On the other hand, there's a telling sentence on the Library of Congress Web site, which states: "The distinction between 'fair use' and infringement may be unclear and not easily defined." The parody of "Oh, Pretty Woman" is a perfect case in point.

It would appear that the court's stance is that the parody in question has to be a parody of the song itself. In other words, the court seems to be saying one can't simply put funny words to the melody of a copyrighted work. One has to be "making fun" of the original song.

Unfortunately, the Supreme Court's decision made the waters murky enough that some judges have used the 2 Live Crew case rather loosely in determining whether or not a work is a parody that enters the fair use arena. Several years after the Supreme Court's ruling, a song in my catalog was used as a sort of intro to a recording artist's otherwise original song. The singer sang the entire first verse of the song in my catalog, changing two of the twenty-seven words in the verse and none of the melody. My co-publishers and I filed a copyright infringement suit against the artist, the record label, and everyone else we could think of. But it was all for naught, because the judge ruled that, since two words were changed, this new version was a parody and was, therefore considered fair use.

I have had another situation in which a record label came to me in advance, claiming that a comedian on their roster was going to be recording a parody version of one of the songs I represented, and that no mechanical royalties would be due since the parody fell into the fair use category. When I asked to see the lyrics, I discovered that the parody lyrics weren't parodying my song. They were actually making fun of a famous country artist whose last name happened to be the same as the name of the song in my catalog. Based on the Supreme Court's ruling, the lyrics had to parody my *song* to fall under fair use. When I wrote back and explained my interpretation of the Supreme Court's decision, the label did a complete about-face and came back to me asking for permission to put out the record with new lyrics. I agreed to let them, as long as they agreed that my company would be the copyright owner of the derivative work and that the full statutory mechanical rate would be paid. I'm happy to report that they complied with my demands. I presume the record label's lawyer saw my point and decided not to challenge my position.

Unfortunately, there have been—and will continue to be—decisions made by various U.S. courts that seem to fly in the face of various sections of the copyright law. As someone once said, "A camel is a horse designed by a committee." The U.S. Copyright Act was designed by a committee, and will, therefore, always be subject to the interpretation of whoever is reading it.

But rather than get bogged down in the law's grayer areas, let's move on to a subject of great importance to both songwriters and music publishers.

The Compulsory Mechanical License

The compulsory mechanical license grants recording companies (and anyone else who wishes) the right to record and release a copyrighted composition without obtaining permission from the copyright owner as long as: (1) an initial release of a phonorecord of the song has already taken place in the United States with the copyright owner's permission, and (2) those subsequently recording and releasing the song on phonorecords adhere to the compulsory mechanical license rules as described in the copyright law.

Compulsory licenses became a part of the Copyright Act in 1909. The 1909 Act said that someone wishing to record and distribute a published musical work via a mechanical device (in those days, the law was referring to piano rolls, cylinder recordings, and early disc recordings) could do so provided that a notice of intention was given and the proper fees were paid to the copyright owner. Under the 1976 law:

> *Any person who wishes to obtain a compulsory license . . . shall, before or within thirty days after making, and before distributing any phonorecords of the work, serve notice of intention to do so on the copyright owner. If the registration or other public records of the Copyright Office do not identify the copyright owner and include an address at which notice can be served, it shall be sufficient to file the notice of intention in the Copyright Office.*

The licensee is also required to make monthly payments to the copyright owner, with an accounting statement rendered "under oath" detailing the number of phonorecords distributed during the previous month.

The 1976 law also outlines other types of compulsory licenses for noncommercial educational broadcasting and for secondary transmissions by cable systems. However, the compulsory license that has the greatest ramifications for songwriters and publishers is the compulsory mechanical license.

This concept was originally created to prevent a monopoly by the Aeolian Co., a piano roll manufacturer that had entered into lengthy and exclusive rights contracts with the major music publishers around the turn of the twentieth century. These contracts gave Aeolian exclusive rights to make piano rolls of the most popular songs of the day, and caused other companies to be cut out of this lucrative business. The compulsory mechanical license that was created by the 1909 Copyright Act gave the other piano roll companies a loophole of sorts through which they could have access to the same popular songs as Aeolian.

The compulsory mechanical license would later prevent any one record company from having an exclusive license to any particular song. Consider for a moment what the situation might be today if the compulsory mechanical license had never been created. If the Beatles' American record label had all of their songs signed to exclusive contracts, a song like "Yesterday" could be recorded only by artists on that particular label. Because of the compulsory mechanical license, hundreds of artists on hundreds of different record labels have recorded "Yesterday," turning it into one of the most popular songs of all time.

There have also been many cases in which songs originally recorded on small labels later became hits because they were released on a major label. For songwriters and music publishers, the importance of the compulsory mechanical license concept can't be overstated.

Although the compulsory mechanical license is invaluable, the procedures involved in its proper implementation (the notice of intention, monthly accountings, etc.) make it quite cumbersome. The many rules involved in properly adhering to the requirements of the compulsory license prompted the creation of the *negotiated mechanical license,* which is used in the music industry today to bypass the complexities of the compulsory mechanical license while still adhering to copyright law.

The negotiated mechanical license isn't a part of the copyright law, but I mention it now because its use has resulted in a major source of music publishing income in modern times. Negotiated mechanical licenses and mechanical royalties will be discussed in detail at the beginning of chapter six.

≈ FOUR ≈

The Intricacies of Copyright Protection

Works Made for Hire

A copyright is created via the process of authorship. The Copyright Act says that ownership of a copyright "vests initially in the author or authors of the work." What all of this means is that the person who writes the song is the initial copyright owner.

The law goes on to say that "the authors of a joint work are co-owners of copyright in the work." In other words, unless the writers have an agreement to the contrary, each writer who contributes to the creation of a particular song is an equal co-owner of that song.

Are there exceptions to these rules? As you have probably surmised by now, exceptions exist throughout the copyright law. In the case of copyright ownership, there is one particularly problematic exception to the general rule that the true author of a work is the initial copyright holder. The exception in this case is something called a *work made for hire*. A work made for hire is defined in the law as "a work prepared by an employee within the scope of his or her employment" or "a work specially ordered or commissioned" for use in one of nine different categories,* if the parties agree in writing that the work is to be for hire, even if the creator is not an employee in the traditional sense.

A while back, I wrote liner notes for a particular record company. Under our agreement, everything I wrote for the company was a work made for hire. Although I was the creator of the work, my employer was the author of the work under the Copyright Act.

As a songwriter, you should generally avoid contracts that describe your songs as works made for hire. However, there are certain times when such a situation is almost unavoidable. Unless you are practically a superstar, if you write a film or television score or a commercial jingle, your efforts will usually be contracted as work made for hire. Also, staff songwriter deals are

---

*For the extremely curious, the nine categories are: (1) as a contribution to a collective work; (2) as a part of a motion picture or other audiovisual work; (3) as a translation; (4) as a supplementary work; (5) as a compilation; (6) as an instructional text; (7) as a test; (8) as answer material for a test; or (9) as an atlas.

sometimes made for hire. Further discussion of issues surrounding work made for hire appears in chapter seven.

Length of Copyright Protection

As you have already learned, the life span of a copyright has changed dramatically over the years. Originally, copyright protection in the U.S. lasted for fourteen years after registration of the copyright, with the term renewable for another fourteen years. By 1976, the length of copyright protection had increased to the life of the author plus fifty years, or *life-plus-fifty*. However, on October 27, 1998, President Clinton signed the Sonny Bono Copyright Term Extension Act into law, extending copyright protection for an additional twenty years, to *life-plus-seventy*.

Therefore, if you are a songwriter whose works have all been created after December 31, 1977, the length of copyright protection for your songs under normal circumstances is from the moment they are created until seventy years after your unfortunate passing. The key phrases here are "after December 31, 1977" and "under normal circumstances." The truth is that there are actually a variety of lengths of copyright protection currently in effect.

What happened to those songs written prior to 1978? Before I attempt to answer that, let's have a quick review of copyright law in effect prior to 1978. Under the 1909 Copyright Act, a copyright lasted for twenty-eight years. During the twenty-eighth year, a renewal had to be filed with the Copyright Office for the copyright to be extended for another twenty-eight years, making the total length of that copyright fifty-six years.

So what happened to all of those pre-1978 songs when the new law went into effect? The renewal term was extended from twenty-eight years to forty-seven years, making the total possible length of a copyright for a pre-1978 song seventy-five years. That is, until the Sonny Bono Copyright Term Extension Act was signed into law. At that point, the forty-seven year term became sixty-seven years, making the new total possible duration of a pre-1978 copyright ninety-five years.

If a copyright was already in renewal, the renewal term was automatically extended to forty-seven years (now sixty-seven years, thanks again to Sonny Bono). But, the 1976 Copyright Act still called for those songs originally copyrighted between January 1, 1950, and December 31, 1977, to have renewal forms filed with the Copyright Office during the twenty-eighth year of copyright for the renewal term to take effect. Otherwise, the copyright would expire at the end of the first twenty-eight years.

In other words, despite the fact that songs being written today have a copyright span of life-plus-seventy, plenty of pre-1978 songs still had to be renewed when those copyrights reached their twenty-eighth year in order to receive the additional years of copyright protection. For example, the song "Jailhouse Rock" was written by Jerry Leiber and Mike Stoller in 1957. In 1985, the twenty-eighth year of the copyright, a Form RE was filed with the Copyright Office, giving the song its extended copyright protection.

On June 26, 1992, Public Law 102-307 was enacted, amending the copyright law to *automatically* extend the term of copyrights secured between January 1, 1964 and December 31, 1977. This law made the filing of the renewal form optional for those works. The huge advantage to

P.L. 102-307 was that copyright owners whose songs were originally copyrighted between 1964 and 1977 no longer had to worry about their songs going into the public domain due to failure to file the proper form.

But, if you wrote your first song on or after January 1, 1978, your copyrights will still be in effect until seventy years after you've gone to rock and roll heaven, right? In almost all cases, the answer is yes. The exceptions are works made for hire and anonymous or pseudonymous works, in which case the length of copyright is either ninety-five years from the date of publication or one hundred and twenty years from the date of creation, whichever expires first. Already you can probably see one of the problems inherent in a work made for hire. Although you most likely won't live to see a work made for hire expire after ninety-five years, your heirs may not be able to enjoy the financial benefits of your work nearly as long as they would have if your creation hadn't been made for hire.

If your copyright is not a work made for hire, and if you write under an assumed name or anonymously, the copyright duration will still be life-plus-seventy if you reveal your real name when you register your songs with the Copyright Office. (See the sample registration form on pages 44-45.)

If you are concerned about your heirs, you might be interested to know that when a song is written by two or more people, the copyright continues to exist for seventy years after the "last surviving author's death." This rule has prompted a few songwriters I know to list their children as co-writers on songs written after 1977. (Whether this practice is legal won't be determined until it is challenged by someone in a court of law.)

The Copyright Notice

There was a time in the not-too-distant past when failure to place a copyright notice on visually perceptible copies of a song meant losing the copyright entirely. Beginning with the original U.S. Copyright Act of 1790, the copyright notice has been an important part of the law. Until the 1976 copyright law was enacted, omitting the copyright notice or putting it in the wrong place on a piece of sheet music could result in the song going into the public domain.

Luckily, the 1976 law was much more reasonable, allowing the failure to include the copyright notice (and other technical errors regarding the notice) to be correctable. If you followed the Copyright Act's "procedures for correcting errors and omissions of the copyright notice on works published on or after January 1, 1978," your copyright would not be lost. The good news today is that the current copyright statute (as amended to comply with the Berne Convention) says that failure to properly affix the copyright notice on a work created on or after March 1, 1989, cannot cause that work to enter the public domain.

So what is this copyright notice and what makes it so important? First of all, if you own sheet music, records, posters, or anything else that is copyrightable, you've seen copyright notices before. It is that familiar little C with a circle around it, followed by the year of copyright and the name of the copyright owner. If you look near the front of this book, you will see a notice that says "© 2005 by Randy Poe."

Here are the Copyright Office's exact specifications for a technically correct copyright notice, should you choose to include one.

1. The symbol ©, or the word *Copyright*, or the abbreviation *Copr.*
2. The year of the first publication of the work.
3. The name of the copyright owner.

This notice should appear on one of the first pages of published works that are visually perceptible. The purpose of this notice is to let the public know that a work is protected by copyright, the year of first publication, and who the copyright owner is. If a copyright notice appears on a copy of a work, the public is being put on notice that this published work can't be copied without permission of the copyright owner (although lack of a notice doesn't mean copying *is* allowed). One would be taking a chance to copy a piece of music just because it doesn't have a copyright notice.

If the current law says you don't have to worry about your song going PD if you leave the copyright notice off, then what's the big deal? The answer is that someone acquiring a copy of your published song with no copyright notice on it might assume that the song is in the public domain. If that person uses your work and can prove that she was misled by the fact that there was no notice, you could suffer the loss of certain damages that might otherwise have been recovered from that party in an infringement suit.

As we've already briefly discussed, the creation of a work is not the same as the publication of that work. The year of *publication* is the year that is listed on the copyright notice. Unpublished works *are* protected under copyright law, however. To protect unpublished works, the Copyright Office suggests that you place a copyright notice on the work, including the words *Unpublished Work* prior to your copyright notice. For example, if I were to write a song today, at the bottom of my lead sheet I could write, "Unpublished Work Copyright 2005 Randy Poe."

Areas Not Protected by Copyright

Original songs that have been "fixed in a tangible form of expression"—written down or otherwise recorded—are protected under federal copyright law. But there are a couple of noncopyrightable areas that pertain to songwriters. Perhaps the most important of these is the *title* of a song. If you write a song called "I Love My Dog," someone else can write another song with the same title. Obviously the lyrics and music will have to be different from yours (with the possible exception of the phrase *I love my dog*), but the fact remains that your song title isn't protected by copyright law.

Does this mean you're free to sit down and write a song called "Rudolph the Red-Nosed Reindeer?" Not really. In the case of a title that has reached the point of having a secondary meaning, laws regarding unfair competition protect it. Unfair competition laws generally prevent someone from attempting to confuse members of the public by making them think that another's property is hers; in other words, by passing off a more notable creation as her own. Since most people would consider "Rudolph the Red-Nosed Reindeer" to be the title of one particular song with the melody and lyrics created by Johnny Marks, the title has become so closely identified with the Johnny Marks composition that it means *only* that song and no other.

So, the public would expect any newly released recording of a song entitled "Rudolph the Red-Nosed Reindeer" to be the one by Johnny Marks. The title has thus acquired a secondary meaning—Johnny Marks's song about one of Santa's reindeer—to the extent that others can be prevented from using it as the title for a different song.

If you keep in mind that one of the major points of writing a song is to create something new and original, you shouldn't have a problem coming up with titles that won't fall into the category of unfair competition.

Another area not protected by copyright is the *idea* for a song. This includes musical and lyrical ideas. There have been thousands of songs with lyrics about a man getting drunk in a bar because his woman left him (or vice versa). Each writer who expresses that idea has a copyright not of the idea, but of her particular expression of it.

Copyright Infringement

My experience in meeting with songwriters early in their careers is that one of their major concerns revolves around the fear of copyright infringement. On the one hand, the rookie songwriter is concerned that she will accidentally copy another songwriter's copyrighted work, while on the other hand, she is concerned that someone else will steal the melody or lyrics of one of her compositions. Before we begin to dwell on these fearful thoughts, let's first find out what copyright infringement actually is—or, rather, what the two most common kinds of copyright infringement are.

The unauthorized use of a copyrighted work is onetype of infringement. For example, if a recording of a copyrighted song is released and no royalties are paid to the copyright owner as required by law, the parties releasing and selling the record can be found guilty of copyright infringement. The owner of an establishment where copyrighted songs are performed in public without permission from the copyright owners or their affiliated performing rights societies is also guilty of copyright infringement. (See chapter eight, entitled Performance Royalties.)

The other kind of copyright infringement is the kind most beginning songwriters are worried about—the unauthorized copying of substantial portions of a work that is protected by copyright law. Dozens of times, novice songwriters have asked me how many measures or notes of a song someone can copy without being guilty of copyright infringement. I'm sorry to have to report that there is no law that stipulates the exact point at which a songwriter has crossed into the area of "substantial similarity." The best way of dealing with this issue is to be original. Don't copy any measures of someone else's song, and you won't have to worry so much about the possibility of infringement.

Of course, the other reason songwriters ask this question is because they feel another party is guilty of infringing one of their original works. This brings up another major point about copyright infringement: For there to be infringement, first there has to be proof of access.

For instance, let's say Bob is a songwriter living in Alaska, and Ray is a songwriter living in Alabama. Bob writes a song and makes a demo of it in May. In June, Ray writes a song that is substantially similar to Bob's song. A copyright exists when a work is put down in a fixed form (written down or recorded, for instance). Therefore, since Bob's copyright became effective in May, Bob has grounds to sue Ray for copyright infringement, right? Wrong!

Why not? Because Ray had no *access* to Bob's song. If he had no way to hear it, he had no way to copy a substantial portion of it (or any of it, for that matter). Therefore, both Bob and Ray have each created individual copyrightable works.

Let's change the story slightly: Bob writes a song in May and sends it to his cousin Joanne in Alabama. Ray goes to a party at Joanne's house, where she plays Bob's song on her CD player. Ray goes home and writes a song, substantially copying Bob's song. Ray figures that Bob is never going to know. He's thousands of miles away.

A few months later, a major star records Ray's song (or, rather, Ray's rewrite of Bob's song). Bob hears the song on the radio, does a little investigating, and soon Bob and Ray are in court. Because the songs are substantially similar, and because Ray had access to Bob's song, Ray is found guilty of copyright infringement (unless, of course, Ray has a very powerful attorney, in which case anything can happen).

Let's change the story one more time: Bob writes a song that becomes a major hit. Ray is also a successful songwriter. Ten years after Bob's song is a hit, Ray writes a song that is substantially similar melodically, but the lyrics are totally different. Ray's song also becomes a big hit. Bob sues Ray for copyright infringement. Ray argues that the similarity between the two songs is strictly a coincidence. He is a successful songwriter and has no need or desire to intentionally copy Bob's melody. In fact, he has no recollection of ever hearing Bob's song. Is Ray found guilty of copyright infringement? After all, there doesn't seem to be any way to prove Ray had access to Bob's song.

The answer is that Ray is guilty (assuming the powerful attorney was unavailable). Since Bob's song was a major hit, no evidence is required to show how Ray gained access to Bob's song. Even if the song had been only a minor hit, access is implied, since the song was widely disseminated to the public. Regarding the fact that Ray obviously copied Bob's melody, the question of whether the copying was done consciously or "subconsciously" does not negate the fact that Ray is guilty.

As you can now surmise, copyright infringement is more than a matter of how many measures of one song are similar to another song. If you are still concerned about someone copying a song you've written, the precautionary measure you should take is obvious: Keep track of everyone you send your demos to. Without evidence that someone had access to your song, you can't prove that she copied it.

Beyond that, your major concern should be to write songs that are original enough that other people won't accuse you of copying their songs.

Publishing Agreements and Published Songs

Now that you've learned a lot about U.S. copyright law, it's time to dig deeper into the definition of music publishing. Consider the following scenario.

Nancy Novice has written a pop song that she feels certain will become better known than the national anthem if she can just get it signed to the right music publisher. Nancy's aunt

A Personal Opinion of the Song Shark

In the scenario between Nancy Novice and Harry Hopeful, I said, "If Harry is a reputable music publisher, he is going to make every effort to get {Nancy's} song recorded by someone." Anyone who has been involved in the music business for more than a few days is aware that there are some disreputable music publishers out there as well. Although there are varying degrees of sleaziness within this disreputable lot, none are worse than those known as *song sharks*.

A song shark is a party that charges songwriters money for certain services. Song sharks place advertisements in practically every kind of magazine, promising the very things unsuspecting songwriters want to be promised. These days, many song sharks have Web sites as well.

You may have seen Web pages or magazine ads in which the advertiser claims he will add music to your poem or lyrics and make a "professional demo." Such advertisements are schemes that usually result in nothing more than a bad piano/vocal demo for which the songwriter is charged an exorbitant fee. The only person who prospers from this type of venture is the song shark himself.

Back about thirty years ago, I learned about song sharks and decided to see just how reprehensible they could be. One day I sat down and wrote some really atrocious lyrics. Then I looked through the classified ads of a popular magazine and found the section headed "Songwriters." I picked an advertisement that had been placed by a music publishing company I'd never heard of before. This particular ad didn't mention money. It simply promised an evaluation of my work. So, I sent my lyrics to the "publishing company" and waited to see what would happen.

A few days later, I got a letter back telling me that said company was very excited about my work. There was even a list of what this company claimed were the best lyrics they had received in the past year. There sat my song, right in the top five titles listed. After I got through laughing, I read the rest of the letter. For "only $850" (and this was in the mid-1970s!) this company promised to become my publisher, add music to my lyrics, and make a demo of the resultant song. There were also the usual promises of airplay, a possible hit, fame, and so on.

Luckily I knew these promises were—to be polite—falsehoods. Needless to say, I didn't respond to the letter. The company even followed up with several more attempts to get my business. With each new letter, my song kept going up the list of the best lyrics they had received. Unfortunately, many unsuspecting people actually fall for these kinds of tactics.

What usually happens is something like this: After the "professional demo" is made, the song shark contacts the songwriter and suggests that a "master recording" be made (for a much higher fee, of course). Then there is money needed to manufacture a thousand CDs. After that, there is money needed for promotion. In some cases, the song shark is able to keep this going even further by convincing the more gullible of his clients to send more lyrics, always promising that a hit record is right around the corner.

In the end, thousands upon thousands of dollars can be spent before the songwriter discovers that nothing is ever really going to happen to further her music career. The truth is, reputable people in the music business just don't do business this way and will have nothing to do with those who carry on such operations.

If you want to avoid disreputable music publishers (and people pretending to be music publishers) the key things to keep in mind are: (1) Real music publishers do not charge money to sign your song. Usually they pay *you* money in the form of an advance. (2) Real music publishers don't charge you a fee to make a demo. Some may take the cost of the demo out of your future royalties, but no money should ever come out of your pocket to make a demo for a song being signed to a publisher. (3) There's no such thing as a mail-order hit. A successful music publisher doesn't solicit songs through the classified section of a magazine or over the Internet. Genuine publishers get so many demos every day that there would be no logical reason to be begging for more from the public at large.

There is no lower form of human life than the person who would take advantage of someone in a helpless situation. In my book, the song shark qualifies as one of the lowest forms of human life imaginable.

knows someone who has a cousin in the music business. After a few phone calls, Nancy is sitting across the desk from a real live music publishing executive named Harry Hopeful. Harry listens to Nancy's song, whips out a contract, and says, "Sign here and your song will be signed to Harry Hopeful Music, Inc."

Nancy signs the contract, goes home and tells all of her friends that she just got her first song published. Everyone congratulates her on her success. Parties are thrown, telegrams are sent, and all of Nancy's friends are talking about how famous Nancy is about to become.

Nancy sits back and waits for the money to start rolling in. Days pass and nothing happens. After a few weeks her friends stop asking her about how well her song is doing. A couple of months pass, and finally Nancy calls Harry Hopeful to find out why it's taking so long for her "published song" to become a hit.

Harry replies, "Well, the song is really good, but I haven't found the right artist to record it yet. These things take time."

"I thought our agreement said that you were publishing my song," whines Nancy.

"Oh, you misunderstood," Harry says. "There's a big difference between signing a publishing contract and having a song published."

So what's the difference? For the answer, let's go back to the Copyright Act's definition of publication. A song isn't published until there has been "distribution of copies or phonorecords of a work to the public by sale . . ." or an "offering to distribute copies or phonorecords to a group of persons for purposes of further distribution, public performance, or public display." When Nancy signed a publishing contract with Harry Hopeful Music, Inc., she was giving Harry *permission* to publish her song. Unless there was a specific clause in her contract stating that Harry had to have sheet music printed and distributed within a specific amount of time (a clause that once existed in contracts during the days when sheet music was the major source of publishing income), Harry was under no obligation to actually *publish* the song.

Obviously, if Harry is a reputable music publisher, he is going to make every effort to get the song recorded by someone. And once the song is recorded and distributed (or there has been an "offering to distribute"), then the song will be a published work.

Until actions have taken place that fulfill the requirements of the Copyright Act's definition of publication, a song isn't published. In Nancy's case, she should have told everyone that her song had been *signed* to a music publisher. After all, that sounds pretty impressive too.

Copyrights, Music Publishing, and the Music Industry

Music publishing—although a vital part of the entertainment industry—has, until recently, taken a back seat to some of the more glamorous aspects of the music business. Perhaps it's the intangibility factor that caused music publishing to be looked down upon by record companies and other segments of the industry.

Another probable cause of its former lack of appeal was the old image of the crude, cigar-chomping music publisher taking advantage of gullible and naive songwriters. The real cause of the industry's attitude was probably a lack of understanding of what publishing is all about. Ignorance always tends to breed suspicion.

These negative attitudes reversed themselves in recent years when the prices publishing catalogs began to bring in the marketplace made the real value of copyrights obvious. Acquisitions and mergers in the publishing industry have shown that there are many millions of dollars to be made. Since the music business *is a business*, the fact that music publishing companies are valuable assets has prompted newfound respect among the other elements that make up the entertainment industry.

Major movie studios, record companies, management firms, booking agencies, promotion companies, and lots of performers have gone out of business, sold for low figures, or gone bankrupt. Music publishing companies, due to their product, would be hard pressed to go bankrupt. It's a fascinating fact, but it's true. Why do music publishers rarely go under? Because copyrights have extremely long life spans. As long as a song is on a recording that is still selling copies, is being performed on radio or television, is being used in a film, or is being sold in sheet music or folio form, the publisher of that song is earning royalties. In fact, a song that may be earning only a few pennies a year can suddenly begin earning hundreds of thousands of dollars if it is recorded by an important artist or used in a nationally broadcast commercial.

For example, a song from the 1950s that was an obscure B side of a hit single may not have earned any royalties since that original hit dropped off the charts. Today, if that same B side is used in a film or recorded by a major artist, it can gain a whole new life that will cause it to earn royalties for years to come. I have seen it happen dozens of times with one publishing company that specializes in songs from the early days of rock and roll.

For record companies the overhead can be extremely high. There are often many employees to pay; product has to be manufactured; thousands of dollars have to be spent in promotion and advertising. The cost of several unsuccessful albums in a row can sometimes bring a record company to its knees.

Meanwhile, the cost to the music publisher of a song on an unsuccessful recording may be no more than the advance paid to the songwriter and the fee for an inexpensive demo. And even though the song may not earn back the songwriter's advance on that particular recording, another recording of the same song by another artist on a different label might sell a million copies. The publisher and the songwriter have the potential to make serious money, while the record company that released the original recording of the song is now stuck with thousands of CDs sitting in a warehouse somewhere.

The Money Issue

If you are the type of songwriter who writes songs only because you want to create great music (and I hope that's your first priority), you may be turned off by all this talk of money. The reason I am emphasizing the money aspects of music publishing is because songwriting might one day become your livelihood (if it isn't already). There is a great deal of money to be made in music publishing. Your knowledge of how that money is earned will give you the opportunity to make sure more of it goes into your pocket than into someone else's.

Although most successful songwriters became so because their goal was to write good songs, I have discovered that almost all songwriters are prolific for a limited amount of time. I have known songwriters whose biggest hits were written in the 1940s, and others who had a string of hits in the 1960s. Very few writers (if any) have been prolific from the 1940s to the present day. The point is, once your period of greatest success is behind you, your income is going to be subject to the agreements you signed at the time. So, although the song should certainly be the most important thing to a songwriter, her business affairs should rank a close second.

⁕ FIVE ⁕

Securing a Copyright

One of the most frequently asked questions among newer songwriters is *How do I copyright my song?* Many people assume that a song doesn't receive copyright protection until they have filled out a form and sent it to the Copyright Office. Under the 1976 Copyright Act, however, a copyright exists as soon as your song is written down, recorded, or otherwise *fixed*. Let's go back to the Copyright Act for a definition of *fixed*.

> A work is "fixed" in a tangible medium of expression when its embodiment in a copy or phonorecord, by or under the authority of the author, is sufficiently permanent or stable to permit it to be perceived, reproduced, or otherwise communicated for a period of more than transitory duration. A work consisting of sounds, images, or both, that are being transmitted, is "fixed" for purposes of this title if a fixation of the work is being made simultaneously with its transmission.

The first thing you learn from this definition is that it's not a good idea to write your songs in disappearing ink. The bottom line here is that once you begin to write your song down on paper or record it in some manner, copyright protection is there. No forms are required.

In fact, the law says, "Copyright protection subsists . . . in original works of authorship fixed in any tangible medium of expression. . . ." In other words, as you write down or record each note, copyright protection is taking effect. It is a rare occasion when a writer sits down and creates three verses, a bridge, and a chorus all at one time. Sometimes it takes days, weeks, months, or longer to finish a song. No matter what stage of completion your song has reached, that portion you have fixed on paper, tape, CD, hard drive, or other medium is already protected by copyright.

The law also says that if an original song not previously fixed is being transmitted (such as in the case of a live broadcast over radio or television), and the song's author is allowing the transmission to be recorded, then a copyright exists by virtue of the fact that the song has been fixed under the definition given above.

Why You Should Register a Copyright

Now that you know your copyright is protected whether you register it or not, the next obvious question is *Why should I bother to register my copyright and pay thirty bucks if it's already protected under law?*

One important reason is that registration allows potential users of your songs to acquire information from the Copyright Office regarding copyright ownership of those works. Of course, there are other sources for this information, such as BMI, ASCAP, or the Harry Fox Agency, as we will discuss later. But there are other important reasons for registration.

Jeffrey S. Sacharow is a prominent entertainment attorney based in Los Angeles. Throughout this book I talk about the importance of having a good entertainment lawyer to help you in areas such as contracts and copyright law. When I have copyright questions of my own, Jeff Sacharow is the attorney I go to for answers. Here's what he has to say about the importance of copyright registration:

Although registering your song is not required in order for your song to be protected under U.S. copyright laws (remember, as soon as you fix your song in a "tangible medium of expression"—pen to paper, keyboard to hard drive etc.—you have protection under U.S. copyright laws) there are reasons why registering your songs make sense.

One reason to register your song is that it helps to prove that you own the song. Now, note that I said it helps *to prove you own the song. Registering your song does not automatically mean that the song is original enough that you could stop someone else from exploiting a song with similar or identical elements to your song—or that you own it. Even though you've registered your song, someone can still claim that your work is based on other songs that have already been written and that it is therefore not sufficiently original to be entitled to copyright protection (this defense is sometimes called the* prior art *defense). Or, they can claim that your song infringed their song. But by registering your song with the U.S. Copyright Office, you do gain an advantage: because the information contained in the copyright application is considered* prima fascia *proof of the facts contained in the application (e.g. the name of the author, the copyright claimant, etc.). 'Prima fascia' proof for purposes of this discussion is a fancy way of saying that if someone claims to own your song, and both you and the other songwriter present the exact same amount of evidence showing how and where the song was written, etc., you would win if your song was registered first—because by registering your song first, the 'burden of proof' shifts to the person challenging the information contained in your registration, and that person would have to produce more evidence than you did to convince the judge that they are right.*

There are also other advantages to registration. For one thing, if you want to sue someone for copyright infringement, your song has to be registered. Also, registration permits the judge (it's up to the judge—it's not automatic) to make the other side pay some or all of your legal bills if you sue someone for copyright infringement and you win. Registering your copyright also allows the judge to award up to $150,000 in statutory damages if he finds that the infringement is willful. Now, before you start spending all of that money in your head for that recording studio you've been dreaming of buying (because you're convinced your girlfriend's brother's band wrote a song that is identical to your big hit)—you should be aware that judges typically are very reluctant to award this penalty.

In order to be entitled to reimbursement of your attorney's fees or statutory damages, you have to register your song within a certain period of time after the song is first published. The scope of that discussion is beyond the scope of this chapter, but if you get to a point where you decide to sue someone for copyright infringement, discuss the timing of the registration with your lawyer.

How to Register a Copyright

Registration of a copyright becomes effective when the Copyright Office receives your Form PA, your check, and copy of the work in the mail. Form PA is the application form created by the Copyright Office for the registration of works that fall into the category of performing arts. (Several different forms have been devised for registration of copyrightable works, but the one used by songwriters and music publishers is Form PA.)

Filling out Form PA is a relatively simple procedure. However, if you don't fill it out exactly as the Copyright Office requires, it will be returned to you with a note explaining what you've omitted or filled out incorrectly. Since it can sometimes take months for your form to be approved and assigned a PA number, it's best to fill it out properly the first time so you don't have to fix your mistakes and wait several more months.

I have filled out a sample of Form PA on pages 44-45 using a fictional song as the work to be registered and using my name as author of the work. Now let's go through the nine sections of Form PA, using this sample as our guide.

Section 1

The first section covers the title of the work, any previous or alternative titles, and the nature of the work. I have entitled the song "She Lied, I Cried," so that's what I've written on line one.

Under *Previous or Alternative Titles*, I have listed the alternate name of my song as "He Lied, I Cried." It's likely that—should my song become a big hit—performers of both genders will want to sing it. By listing this obvious alternative title, it will be much easier for those searching for the registration to find my song even if they only know it by its alternative title.

The last line of Section 1, *Nature of This Work*, is simple. My song consists of both words and music, so the proper description is "words and music." If my song had been an instrumental piece, I would have written "music" on this line. If I had only written lyrics for which no melody had yet been composed, I would have written the phrase "song lyrics." You get the idea.

Section 2

The second section of the form requires information about the author(s) of the work. According to the instructions for this form (which are available when you download the form from the Copyright Office Web site), the Copyright Office wants "the fullest form of the author's name," so I've written "William Randall Poe." Under *Dates of Birth and Death*, I have listed the year I was born. Luckily, I get to leave the other half blank. If, in fact, a Form PA were being filled out for a song by a deceased writer, it would be necessary to list the year of death so that the length of copyright protection could be properly determined.

As you will remember from the discussion in chapter four, a work made for hire is "a work prepared by an employee within the scope of his or her employment" or a work commissioned as one of the nine work-made-for-hire categories listed on page 30. My song is not a work made for hire, so I have checked *No* under the question *Was this contribution to the work a "work made for hire"?*

Next comes *Author's Nationality or Domicile*. I've written "U.S.A." on the appropriate line. The form also asks if the work is anonymous or pseudonymous. Since I want everyone to know I wrote "She Lied, I Cried," I've checked *No* for each question.

Had I wished to remain anonymous, I would have checked the *Yes* box. Under *Name of Author*, I would have either: (1) left the line blank; (2) written "Anonymous" on the line; or (3) written my full name, making sure that I had checked *Yes* in the appropriate box. The life of the copyright of an anonymous author has the potential to be much shorter than a copyright in which the true name of the author has been revealed.

If I had written the song using the pseudonym Muddy Johnson, I would have checked *Yes* where appropriate on the form. My choices under *Name of Author* would have been to: (1) leave the line blank; (2) write my pseudonym and indicate it as such ("Muddy Johnson, pseudonym"); or (3) write my real name and my pseudonym, making sure I had clearly indicated which was which ("William Randall Poe, whose pseudonym is Muddy Johnson"). Once again, in certain circumstances, using a pseudonym can shorten the life of the copyright. Keep in mind that whether you use your real name, use a pseudonym, or remain anonymous, you still have to list your citizenship or domicile.

The last line of Section 2a is *Nature of Authorship*. Since I wrote the song by myself, I put "words and music" here. If I had written just the words and someone else had composed the music, my line would say "words" and my co-writer's line (in Section 2b) would say "music." If both of us had contributed to the lyrics and melody of the song, we would each be listed as "co-author of words and music."

SECTION 3

The third section of Form PA involves creation and publication. We already know that a copyright is created when it's fixed for the first time in some tangible medium or on a phonorecord. In the case of my song, I wrote the music in 2004 and the lyrics in 2005. Since I am registering the completed version of my song, I have written 2005 as the year of creation.

My song hasn't been published yet (or my publisher would probably be filling out this form instead of me), so I left the *First Publication* section (3b) blank. At the beginning of chapter two, we discussed what constitutes a published work. If, say, a commercial recording of my song had been distributed beginning on February 1, 2005, that would be the date listed as *First Publication of This Particular Work*. Assuming this was initially a domestic release, the *Nation of First Publication* would be "U.S.A."

SECTION 4

Section 4 requires the name and address of the *Copyright Claimant(s)*. Since I wrote the song alone and have not assigned, sold, or transferred it to another party, I have listed my own name and address. Under *Transfer*, I have left the line blank.

Copyright Office fees are subject to change.
For current fees, check the Copyright Office
website at www.copyright.gov, write the Copyright Office, or call (202) 707-3000.

Form PA
For a Work of Performing Arts
UNITED STATES COPYRIGHT OFFICE

REGISTRATION NUMBER

PA _____ PAU

EFFECTIVE DATE OF REGISTRATION

_____ Month _____ Day _____ Year

DO NOT WRITE ABOVE THIS LINE. IF YOU NEED MORE SPACE, USE A SEPARATE CONTINUATION SHEET.

1

TITLE OF THIS WORK ▼

SHE LIED, I CRIED

PREVIOUS OR ALTERNATIVE TITLES ▼

HE LIED, I CRIED

NATURE OF THIS WORK ▼ See instructions

WORDS AND MUSIC

2

a NAME OF AUTHOR ▼

WILLIAM RANDALL POE

DATES OF BIRTH AND DEATH
Year Born ▼ 1955 Year Died ▼

Was this contribution to the work a "work made for hire"?
☐ Yes
☑ No

AUTHOR'S NATIONALITY OR DOMICILE
Name of Country
OR { Citizen of USA
{ Domiciled in _____

WAS THIS AUTHOR'S CONTRIBUTION TO THE WORK
Anonymous? ☐ Yes ☑ No
Pseudonymous? ☐ Yes ☑ No
If the answer to either of these questions is "Yes," see detailed instructions.

NATURE OF AUTHORSHIP Briefly describe nature of material created by this author in which copyright is claimed. ▼
WORDS AND MUSIC

NOTE

Under the law, the "author" of a "work made for hire" is generally the employer, not the employee (see instructions). For any part of this work that was "made for hire" check "Yes" in the space provided, give the employer (or other person for whom the work was prepared) as "Author" of that part, and leave the space for dates of birth and death blank.

b NAME OF AUTHOR ▼

DATES OF BIRTH AND DEATH
Year Born ▼ Year Died ▼

Was this contribution to the work a "work made for hire"?
☐ Yes
☐ No

AUTHOR'S NATIONALITY OR DOMICILE
Name of Country
OR { Citizen of _____
{ Domiciled in _____

WAS THIS AUTHOR'S CONTRIBUTION TO THE WORK
Anonymous? ☐ Yes ☐ No
Pseudonymous? ☐ Yes ☐ No
If the answer to either of these questions is "Yes," see detailed instructions.

NATURE OF AUTHORSHIP Briefly describe nature of material created by this author in which copyright is claimed. ▼

c NAME OF AUTHOR ▼

DATES OF BIRTH AND DEATH
Year Born ▼ Year Died ▼

Was this contribution to the work a "work made for hire"?
☐ Yes
☐ No

AUTHOR'S NATIONALITY OR DOMICILE
Name of Country
OR { Citizen of _____
{ Domiciled in _____

WAS THIS AUTHOR'S CONTRIBUTION TO THE WORK
Anonymous? ☐ Yes ☐ No
Pseudonymous? ☐ Yes ☐ No
If the answer to either of these questions is "Yes," see detailed instructions.

NATURE OF AUTHORSHIP Briefly describe nature of material created by this author in which copyright is claimed. ▼

3

a YEAR IN WHICH CREATION OF THIS WORK WAS COMPLETED This information must be given in all cases.
2005 Year

b DATE AND NATION OF FIRST PUBLICATION OF THIS PARTICULAR WORK
Complete this information ONLY if this work has been published.
Month _____ Day _____ Year _____ Nation

4

COPYRIGHT CLAIMANT(S) Name and address must be given even if the claimant is the same as the author given in space 2. ▼

WILLIAM RANDALL POE
461 OCEAN BOULEVARD, MALIBU, CA 98765-4321

See instructions before completing this space.

TRANSFER If the claimant(s) named here in space 4 is (are) different from the author(s) named in space 2, give a brief statement of how the claimant(s) obtained ownership of the copyright. ▼

APPLICATION RECEIVED

ONE DEPOSIT RECEIVED

TWO DEPOSITS RECEIVED

FUNDS RECEIVED

DO NOT WRITE HERE OFFICE USE ONLY

MORE ON BACK ▶ • Complete all applicable spaces (numbers 5-9) on the reverse side of this page.
• See detailed instructions. • Sign the form at line 8.

DO NOT WRITE HERE
Page 1 of _____ pages

EXAMINED BY	FORM PA
CHECKED BY	
☐ CORRESPONDENCE Yes	FOR COPYRIGHT OFFICE USE ONLY

DO NOT WRITE ABOVE THIS LINE. IF YOU NEED MORE SPACE, USE A SEPARATE CONTINUATION SHEET.

PREVIOUS REGISTRATION Has registration for this work, or for an earlier version of this work, already been made in the Copyright Office?

☐ Yes ☑ No If your answer is "Yes," why is another registration being sought? (Check appropriate box.) ▼ If your answer is No, do **not** check box A, B, or C.

a. ☐ This is the first published edition of a work previously registered in unpublished form.

b. ☐ This is the first application submitted by this author as copyright claimant.

c. ☐ This is a changed version of the work, as shown by space 6 on this application.

If your answer is "Yes," give: **Previous Registration Number** ▼   **Year of Registration** ▼

5

DERIVATIVE WORK OR COMPILATION Complete both space 6a and 6b for a derivative work; complete only 6b for a compilation.
Preexisting Material Identify any preexisting work or works that this work is based on or incorporates. ▼

a

6

See instructions before completing this space.

Material Added to This Work Give a brief, general statement of the material that has been added to this work and in which copyright is claimed. ▼

b

DEPOSIT ACCOUNT If the registration fee is to be charged to a Deposit Account established in the Copyright Office, give name and number of Account.
Name ▼   **Account Number** ▼

a

7

CORRESPONDENCE Give name and address to which correspondence about this application should be sent. Name/Address/Apt/City/State/ZIP ▼

WILLIAM RANDALL POE
461 OCEAN BOULEVARD
MALIBU, CA 98765-4321

b

Area code and daytime telephone number (310) 555-1234   Fax number (310) 555-4321

Email NAME@COMPANY.COM

CERTIFICATION* I, the undersigned, hereby certify that I am the

Check only one ▶

☑ author
☐ other copyright claimant
☐ owner of exclusive right(s)
☐ authorized agent of _____
Name of author or other copyright claimant, or owner of exclusive right(s) ▲

of the work identified in this application and that the statements made by me in this application are correct to the best of my knowledge.

8

Typed or printed name and date ▼ If this application gives a date of publication in space 3, do not sign and submit it before that date.

WILLIAM RANDALL POE _____ Date **9/22/2005**

Handwritten signature (X) ▼

x _William Randall Poe_

9

| Certificate
will be
mailed in
window
envelope
to this
address: | Name ▼
WILLIAM RANDALL POE

Number/Street/Apt ▼
461 OCEAN BOULEVARD

City/State/ZIP ▼
MALIBU, CA 98765-4321 | **YOU MUST:**
• Complete all necessary spaces
• Sign your application in space 8
**SEND ALL 3 ELEMENTS
IN THE SAME PACKAGE:**
1. Application form
2. Nonrefundable filing fee in check or money
order payable to *Register of Copyrights*
3. Deposit material
MAIL TO:
Library of Congress
Copyright Office
101 Independence Avenue, S.E.
Washington, D.C. 20559-6000 | Fees are subject to
change. For current
fees, check the
Copyright Office
website at
www.copyright.gov,
write the Copyright
Office, or call
(202) 707-3000. |

*17 U.S.C. § 506(e): Any person who knowingly makes a false representation of a material fact in the application for copyright registration provided for by section 409, or in any written statement filed in connection with the application, shall be fined not more than $2,500.

Rev: June 2002—20,000 Web Rev: June 2002 ♻ Printed on recycled paper

U.S. Government Printing Office: 2000-461-113/20,021

If I had signed an agreement with a music publisher for "She Lied, I Cried," the publisher would, in most cases, be listed as the *Copyright Claimant*, and the words "by written contract" (or a similar phrase) would be listed under *Transfer*.

Section 5

Section 5 pertains to any "previous registration" of the copyright. On my application I've checked *No* because this is my first registration of the song. The reasons why there would be a need for registering the copyright a second time include listing an additional author as a copyright claimant or registering a "changed version of the work."

Earlier, I said that I had written the music to my song in 2004 and added the lyrics in 2005. If I had registered the copyright when it was still an instrumental piece, I would now need to register the work again because it would fall into the category of a "changed version of the work."

Section 6

The sixth section is for a song that is a derivative work or compilation, or for a song that is a "changed version." I have left this section blank because it doesn't pertain to my song. If the melody to "She Lied, I Cried" had been partially an original work by me and partially based on the tune of Offenbach's Barcarolle in D Major from the opera *Les Contes d'Hoffman*, I would have indicated that fact on line 6a. On the line for 6b I would have written "new words added; partial revision of melody."

Section 7

The first half of Section 7 is for those who register copyrights so frequently that they have established an account with the Copyright Office. I have left the first half of this section blank because I don't have an account. Instead, I will send a check for thirty dollars along with the application and a recording of "She Lied, I Cried." If I wanted to, I could send a lead sheet of the song rather than a recording.

The second half of Section 7 requests that you give your contact information. For a variety of reasons (if I filled out this application incorrectly, or if I forgot to include my check or my CD, for instance), the Copyright Office needs to know how to contact me.

Section 8

In Section 8, I have checked the box to indicate that I am filing for copyright as the author. I have also typed my name and the date, and have signed the application on the appropriate line.

Section 9

Section 9 is for the name and address of the person to whom the certificate should be mailed. Once the Copyright Office has processed your Form PA, it will be assigned a number and returned to you.

Registering Several Songs at Once

Now that you know how to register one song using Form PA, it's time for me to let you in on a relatively little-known secret for saving money by registering several songs at a time. After all, if you're a prolific songwriter with dozens of songs to register, the process of registering them one at a time can become a pretty expensive enterprise—and the Copyright Office doesn't offer volume discounts!

The fee for registering Form PA is currently thirty dollars.* By filing an additional document—Form CA, which costs one hundred dollars—you can register several songs at once. If you'd rather pay a hundred and thirty bucks instead of six hundred bucks to register twenty songs, here's the trick.

On Form PA, instead of listing one song on the *Title of This Work* line, write a phrase that describes the group of songs you wish to register. For instance, if I have twelve songs to register, I can entitle my work "A Dozen by Randy Poe, Volume One." Any phrase that describes the collection will do: "Songs from the Winter of 2006," "Forty Love Songs," "Songs Written on the A-Train While Commuting to Work." The idea is to give your group of songs a collective title.

When you register an unpublished song, you must include a lead sheet or recording of the work. When registering a collection of songs, you should either: (1) make a CD that contains all of the songs in the collection, or (2) put all of the lead sheets in the collection in an orderly manner by either fastening them together or binding them in a folder.

Anytime something seems less expensive than it should be, there are usually a few strings attached. This method of registering a collection of songs is no exception. To be able to register more than one song on Form PA, all of the songs must: (1) have the same copyright claimant or claimants, and (2) be by the same author (or, if there is more than one author, at least one of the authors has to have written part of every song in the collection). If your songs still qualify, then your next step is to mail in your Form PA with the appropriate fee and materials and wait for your registration certificate to return.

Once it arrives, you will have a PA number, and you'll be ready for part two: Form CA. The CA stands for *Correction/Amplification*. The purpose of filing this form is to amplify the information given on your Form PA.

On Form CA you will need to write the title of your collection, the Form PA registration number, and the year of basic registration, as well as the name(s) of the author(s) and the name(s) of the copyright claimant(s). Under the section for *Amplified Information*, you will list all of the individual song titles that make up your collection. When Form CA is being used to amplify a Form PA, the same person who signed the PA must also sign the CA form.

When you've completed Form CA, send it to the Copyright Office along with a hundred dollars, and you will have successfully registered an entire collection of songs for a total of a hundred and thirty bucks. When the Copyright Office receives your Form CA, it will cross-

*The only things certain in life are death, taxes, and the fact that the cost of registering a copyright will continue to escalate. Read the copyright form carefully and make sure you know the current cost of registration before you send in the form. Otherwise, it'll be winging its way back to you faster than you can say *runaway inflation*.

reference the collection with the titles of the songs listed on the form, which is the equivalent of having registered each song individually. The money you save will go a long way toward making that next demo.

But wait! If you're the sole writer of all the songs in the collection, the Copyright Office has recently devised a registration method that's even cheaper still. It's called the Short Form PA. There are several qualifications you must meet to use the Short Form PA, but if all of them apply to you and your songs, then it's definitely the way you'll want to go.

To use the Short Form PA, you must be the only author and only copyright owner of the songs in the collection; none of the songs can be a work made for hire; the songs must be completely original (no derivative works of any kind allowed); the songs must be unpublished; and you can't use a pseudonym.

If you and your songs meet all of these specifications, fill out the Short Form PA, once again giving a name to your collection and entering it on the line for *Title of This Work*. Fill out the rest of the form (it's just like the regular Form PA—except shorter, of course), and then use Form CON (*CON* stands for *Continuation*) to list each song title individually. Send in the Short Form PA, Form CON, your CD or bound collection of lead sheets, and thirty dollars. The end result will be a certificate of registration that lists the individual song titles as well as the collection title.

I know what you're thinking: *Why didn't Randy use the short form when he was showing me how to register a song?* In truth, I could have, since I was the sole writer of "She Lied, I Cried." However, I wanted to show you how to use the more detailed Form PA, and I also wanted you to see that there is space for three writers on Form PA. By the way, if you write a song with three or more people, Form CON can also be used to list the remaining writers.

How to Get Copyright Forms

Now that you know how to fill out copyright forms, you'll need a few blank forms of your own. If you aren't shy around answering machines, you can get forms quickly by calling the Copyright Office hotline at (202) 707-9100. When you call, you'll get an answering machine that will instruct you to leave your name, address, and the type and number of forms you want. Be sure to speak slowly and spell anything that might be easily misspelled. You can order more than one form at a time, but it's best to order only the amount you need, plus a few extras for additional songs you may wish to register in the near future. My experience with the hotline is that the response time is very short. I have frequently received forms within three days after I ordered them.

You can also order informational circulars put out by the Copyright Office using the hotline number. Circular 1 is entitled "Copyright Basics"; Circular 4 tells you the latest copyright fees; Circular 9 explains "Work-Made-for-Hire Under the 1976 Copyright Act." In true government fashion, the list goes on forever.

Luckily, the Copyright Office also has a site on the Internet (copyright.gov) where you can download all of the forms and circulars you could possibly want. Just be sure to follow all of the directions when it comes to printing out copyright forms downloaded from the Web site. If you'd prefer, there's a page on the site that allows you to order up to five copies of any form and have them mailed to you.

A Final Word on Copyright Registration

When I first got into the business of music publishing over twenty years ago, filing a Form PA cost much, much less than it does today. The Copyright Office has been forced to raise its fees on a continual basis to keep up with the overhead involved in processing all of the registrations that come in.

As Jeff Sacharow points out, "Before you race out tomorrow to register all of your songs, you should be aware that, because registration can be so costly, most publishers typically don't register their songs until after a recording of that song is released. Partly it's a cost issue, and partly—at least with the bigger publishers—it's because their administration departments are already swimming in an ocean of work."

Ultimately, the decision of whether to register your songs prior to their becoming published works is yours to make. If it's within your budget and will help you to sleep better at night, then my advice would be that you should register your songs—keeping in mind that registering a group of them at once as a collection will make the cost of registration less painful.

PART THREE
Royalties

⤜ SIX ⤛

Mechanical Royalties

This section of the book could more precisely be called *the money chapters*. It's time to put away those "root of all evil" feelings that may still be lurking in your conscience and accept the fact that one of the primary functions of a music publisher is to turn a healthy profit. The two main reasons I have written this book are to teach you about the business of music publishing and to help you, as a songwriter, make at least as much money on your songs as your publisher will.

This chapter and the ones to follow will fill you in on all of the major ways music publishers and songwriters receive income: mechanical royalties, synchronization royalties, performance royalties, royalties for grand rights uses, print royalties, "new technology" royalties, and royalties from foreign sources. (Some of these terms are probably beginning to sound familiar to you. Slowly but surely, you're learning the language of the music publishing business.)

Mechanical Royalties

Mechanical royalties are monies paid by a record company for the right to manufacture and distribute phonorecords containing a song owned by the publisher. The amount of money to be paid per unit is usually either: (1) the current statutory mechanical rate, or (2) a reduced rate negotiated by the record company and the music publisher, generally based on a percentage of the statutory mechanical rate.

Okay, I know I've thrown in a bunch of new terms in the course of a couple of sentences, so here are a few definitions and explanations. By now the word *phonorecords* has popped up enough times that you know it means compact discs as well as any similar devices that are now known or created in the future.

The phrase *per unit* refers to the total number of phonorecords in question. If a label manufactures and distributes ten thousand CDs, each of those CDs is one unit.

The *statutory mechanical rate* is the amount of money that the record company owes the music publisher for each unit manufactured and distributed as long as no *reduced rate* has been agreed to by the two parties.

In chapter three we discussed the *compulsory mechanical license* that was originally created under the 1909 Copyright Act and then expanded upon in the 1976 law. This license gives companies that wish to reproduce songs mechanically the right to do so without having to obtain the permission of the copyright owner (as long as phonorecords of the song have previously been distributed to the public in the United States under the copyright owner's authority). The compulsory mechanical license, rules regarding royalty payments require the record company to make those payments to the copyright owner on a monthly basis, provide monthly accountings, and pay the statutory mechanical rate based on the number of phonorecords manufactured and distributed.

A *negotiated mechanical license* is a variation on the compulsory mechanical license. Generally known in the music industry simply as a *mechanical license*, this license is more lenient than a compulsory mechanical license, usually requiring payments on a quarterly basis (as opposed to monthly), sometimes requiring payments to be made only on phonorecords sold (instead of on the total number of recordings manufactured and distributed), and sometimes allowing for a reduced royalty rate (as opposed to the statutory mechanical rate). A compulsory mechanical license doesn't require permission from the copyright owner to manufacture and distribute records, but a negotiated mechanical license does by virtue of the fact that the license must be negotiated between the record company and the copyright owner.

A mechanical license, then, is a negotiated license granting a particular record company permission to manufacture and distribute a recording that contains a song owned by a particular music publisher without having to follow the strict guidelines of a compulsory (nonnegotiable) mechanical license.

When the 1976 Copyright Act was created, a five-person panel called the Copyright Royalty Tribunal (CRT) was put into place. These five people, appointed by the President and confirmed by the Senate, were empowered to (among other things) determine the amount of the statutory mechanical rate.

In the first ten years following the implementation of the 1976 Copyright Act, the statutory mechanical rate was increased several times over. In 1987, a more detailed mathematical formula for determining the amount of future increases was jointly devised by the National Music Publishers' Association (NMPA), the Songwriters Guild of America (SGA), and the Recording Industry Association of America (RIAA). That formula—based on, among other things, changes in the Consumer Price Index—was then adopted by the Copyright Royalty Tribunal.

> In most record companies, there is a battle constantly being fought between the creative forces and the bean counters.

However, as you are quickly learning, copyright law goes through changes seemingly as fast as a baby goes through diapers, because on December 17, 1993, Congress abolished the Copyright Royalty Tribunal, and created the Copyright Arbitration Royalty Panel (CARP) to determine the statutory mechanical rate.

In 1997, a mechanical rate adjustment proceeding was held to determine the rates through 2006. This resulted in the current rate (on the day I'm writing this in 2005) of either 8.5 cents or 1.65 cents per minute, whichever is larger. The next increase will go into effect on January 1, 2006, at which time the rate will become 9.1 cents for songs five minutes long or less, and 1.75 cents per minute (or fraction thereof) for songs over five minutes.

After having first devised the CRT, and then later having replaced the CRT with the CARP system, Congress more recently enacted the Copyright Royalty and Distribution Reform Act of

2004. This act phased out CARP, replacing it with three Copyright Royalty Judges (CRJ). The CRJs are full-time employees of the Library of Congress who will be responsible for determining future changes in the statutory mechanical rate. Just like copyright registration fees, the statutory mechanical royalty rate will most likely continue to rise.

Reduced Rates

Now let's get back to our definitions of terms. A *reduced rate* is a mechanical rate negotiated between a record company and a music publisher (the copyright owner) in which the two parties agree to a lower royalty rate per unit than the statutory mechanical rate.

The most common of these reduced rates is referred to as a *three-quarter rate*, a payment of 75 percent of the current statutory mechanical rate. In other words, if the current statutory rate is 8.5 cents, a record company might agree to pay a three-quarter rate of 6.375 cents per unit (75 percent of 8.5 cents). Although the three-quarter rate is the most commonly negotiated rate, I have seen instances in which the reduced rate was anywhere from 50 percent to 87.5 percent.

Because the statutory mechanical rate continues to go up, it is in the publisher's best interest to contract for a percentage of the statutory mechanical rate rather than for a specific, fixed sum per unit. If, in 2004, a publisher agreed to a reduced rate of 6.375 cents (as opposed to 75 percent of the statutory rate), the publisher would continue to make only 6.375 cents per unit after January 1, 2006, while the publisher who negotiated a three-quarter rate in 2004 would begin making 6.825 cents per unit in 2006.

Determination of the amount of the reduced rate (if it is to be reduced at all) is usually based on how badly the record company needs to use the song in relation to how badly the music publisher wants the song to be used. Let's say, for example, that an artist is in the studio trying to decide which of two songs to record. The album needs only one more number to wrap it up, and everyone agrees that either song will work. Budgetary concerns—studio time, musicians' fees, arrangement costs, production costs, and so forth—are at the top of everyone's mind. Now might be a good time for the record company to contact the songs' publishers and see if either of them will grant a reduced rate. If neither of them will, the record company will have to use some other factor to determine which song to record. (Of course, the same problem applies if both publishers agree to a three-quarter rate.) However, if one publisher says yes to a reduced rate and the other doesn't, it's a pretty safe bet that the record company will go with the song belonging to the publisher who grants the reduced rate.

Just look at the numbers: If the statutory rate is 9.1 cents per unit, and the record company manufactures and distributes one million units, the record company will owe the publisher 9.1 cents times one million—a total of $91,000. On a three-quarter rate basis, using the same million units, the record company owes the publisher $68,250—a savings to the record company of $22,750.

Unfortunately, unless there are spies filling the publisher in on what's really happening at the record company, the publisher may not know the true reason why the record company is asking for a reduced rate. The publisher has to ask herself several questions: *Will the record company go with another song if I don't grant a reduced rate? If I grant a reduced rate on this song,*

Sample Mechanical License

To: Date:

Refer to provisions of this agreement listed below, which vary the terms of the compulsory license provision of the Copyright Act. The following is supplementary thereto:

1.   Song Title:
2.   Songwriter(s) Name(s):
3.   Publisher:
4.   Phonorecord Number:
5.   Playing Time:
6.   Artist:
7.   Format:
8.   Title of Album [if applicable]:
9.   Royalty Rate:
10. Date of Release:

This Agreement is limited to the United States, its territories and possessions.

You have advised us that you wish to obtain a compulsory license to make and distribute phonorecords of the copyrighted work referred to herein, under the compulsory license provision of Section 115 of the Copyright Act.

Upon your doing so, you shall have all the rights which are granted to, and all obligations which are imposed upon, users of said copyrighted work under the compulsory license provision of the Copyright Act, after phonorecords of the copyrighted work have been distributed to the public in the United States under the authority of the copyright owner by another party, except that with respect to phonorecords thereof made and distributed hereunder:

1. You shall pay royalties and account to us quarterly, within forty-five (45) days after the end of each calendar quarter, on the basis of net phonorecords made and distributed;

2. For such phonorecords made and distributed, the royalty shall be the rate stated above;

3. This compulsory license covers and is limited to one particular recording of said copyrighted work as performed by the artist and on the phonorecord number identified above; and this compulsory license does not supersede nor in any way affect any prior agreements now in effect respecting phonorecords of said copyrighted work;

4. Proper writer and publisher credit (i.e., the name[s] of the writer[s] and publisher of said copyrighted work) shall be included on each and every copy of all such phonorecords covered by this license;

5. In the event you fail to account to us and pay royalties as herein provided for, we may give written notice to you that, unless the default is remedied within thirty (30) days of your receipt of the notice, this compulsory license will be automatically terminated. Such termination shall render either the making or the distribution, or both, of all phonorecords for which royalties have not been paid, actionable as acts of infringement under, and fully subject to the remedies provided by, the Copyright Act;

6. You need not serve or file the notice of intention to obtain a compulsory license required by the Copyright Act;

7. We, or our designees, shall have the right to audit your books and records with respect to statements rendered pursuant to this license during regular business hours at your office.

Very Truly Yours,

By: _____
      Publisher

We acknowledge the receipt of a copy hereof and the accuracy of the terms contained herein:

By: _____
      Recording Company

are my chances better at getting another song on a future album for this record company? Do I owe someone at the record company a favor? If the answer to one of these questions is yes, it might be in the publisher's best interest to grant a reduced rate.

However, there are cases in which the record company is simply fishing for a reduced rate. For instance, a publisher might get a request for a reduced rate on a song when the album is already finished and about to be released. You might be surprised to discover that record companies don't always contact the publisher *before* a song is recorded. In most record companies, there is a battle constantly being fought between the creative forces and the bean counters. If an artist wants to record a particular song, the decision to do so might occur in a recording studio at two in the morning—when there is no record company executive around to say, "Wait! Don't spend thousands of dollars in studio time and musician costs until we can find out if the publisher will grant a reduced rate."

The creation of compilation albums can also put the publisher at an advantage over the record company. If a record company plans to put out an album of the fifteen greatest hits of 1957, and I own the publishing rights to one of the top ten songs from that year, I can refuse to grant a reduced rate. It is a relatively safe assumption that my song will have to be included on the album despite the record company's threats to leave it off.

Of course, reason usually prevails among publishers in these situations. Some giant publishing companies will grant a reduced rate at the drop of a hat because they are dealing in such large volume. Smaller publishers tend to be more conservative and cautious. If a publisher has only twenty songs in her catalog, her decision may increase or reduce her company's annual income by a large percentage.

This, then, is yet another area of publishing that isn't cut and dried. There is actual gamesmanship going on between the record company and the music publisher that can mean a substantial difference in the amount of money one makes and the other doesn't.

ENTER THE HARRY FOX AGENCY

The Harry Fox Agency, based in New York City, acts as a licensing organization/collection agency for music publishers. A subsidiary of the National Music Publishers' Association, the Harry Fox Agency (HFA) provides licensing services to thousands of publishers, issuing mechanical licenses to record companies and collecting mechanical royalties on behalf of the publishers. In return for issuing mechanical licenses, HFA charges publishers (and, consequently, songwriters) a commission fee—currently 6.75 percent off the top on royalties HFA collects from record companies.

Let's go back to our hypothetical million-unit sale that, at a mechanical rate of 9.1 cents per unit, would earn the publisher a gross of $91,000. The publisher might pay half of the $91,000 ($45,500) to the songwriter. If the Harry Fox Agency collects the mechanical royalties for those million units, it will take a commission fee of $6,142.50 (6.75 percent of $91,000), leaving the publisher with a gross of $84,857.50, from which the writer will be paid $42,428.75 (half of $84,857.50). The publisher and the songwriter each end up with $3,071.25 less than what the record company paid to HFA.

So why doesn't the music publishing company issue its own mechanical licenses and save the 6.75 percent? Well, some do. However, a major function of HFA is to conduct audits of record companies all over the country, finding unpaid money due to publishers and distributing these recoveries to whomever royalties are owed. In its promotional literature, the National Music Publishers' Association points out that, in many cases, the Harry Fox Agency distributes recoveries that more than compensate for the commission the publishers pay for HFA's services.

Every music publishing company has to decide whether using the Harry Fox Agency makes sense financially in her particular case. Larger publishers with thousands of copyrights might issue many licenses every day. The HFA may be better equipped to handle this heavy workload, and its commission will probably turn out to be less than the cost to the publisher of hiring additional people to do this work.

For a smaller company with only a handful of songs, it might make more sense for the publisher to issue licenses herself. However, collecting monies owed from a record company on the other side of the country can become a costly exercise. Auditing that company can be an expensive proposition also.

Once again, every publisher's case is different. Ultimately, each publisher must decide for herself whether using the Fox Agency is financially beneficial.

Mechanical Royalties in Action

So far in this chapter you've learned about the statutory mechanical rate, reduced rates, gamesmanship in the music business, the Harry Fox Agency, and mechanical licenses—all of which pertain to one of the main sources of the music publisher's income: mechanical royalties. Now let's set up some scenarios and see how all of these things fit together.

SCENARIO NUMBER ONE

Britney Superseller has just recorded an album's worth of material. Being a songwriter, she has composed eleven of the twelve songs, but the twelfth is a song owned by Sam's Smalltime Music Publishing Company.

Sam doesn't use the Harry Fox Agency, so Ed Promo, an executive from Ms. Superseller's record company, contacts Sam directly, telling him that the song will be on the album if Sam will grant a three-quarter rate.

Sam knows that Britney Superseller's last four albums have sold well over a million copies each. A little math tells him that 25 percent of 9.1 cents times one million units is $22,750. So, it's up to Sam to decide whether to say yes to the reduced rate and lose a potential additional profit of $22,750, or to say no and face the possibility of making nothing at all if the record company replaces his song with somebody else's.

Not owning thousands of copyrights, Sam decides not to gamble and agrees to the three-quarter rate. So, Sam issues a mechanical license to the record company. His license calls for payments for the quarters ending March 31, June 30, September 30 and December 31, just as the Fox Agency's license does.

In the music industry, record companies are usually allowed forty-five days after the end of each quarter to make royalty payments. Since Britney Superseller is on a major label with a

The National Music Publishers' Association
(Or, Who Was Harry Fox?)

Formed as the Music Publishers' Protective Association in 1917, the National Music Publishers' Association (NMPA) protects and advances the interests of music publishers in the United States.

In its early days, the organization campaigned for changes in the copyright law. Representatives of the NMPA helped to make up the panel that studied the important changes being proposed in the mid-1950s when Congress began to consider revisions in the 1909 Copyright Act. As discussed in chapter two, the law was finally revised in 1976, with additional changes taking place in 1989 when the United States joined the Berne Convention (as well as other changes both major and minor that have taken place since 1989. To list every single change made in the U.S. copyright law between 1976 and 2005 would fill a book—and it wouldn't be nearly as much fun to read as this one).

As copyrighted music began to be used in films, NMPA created a service that issued synchronization licenses on behalf of all music publishers who wished to use the organization as their licensing agent. In charge of this service was NMPA's chairman of the board, E. Claude Mills. In 1936, the NMPA added the licensing of electrical transcriptions of radio programs to its list of services to publishers. Two years later, a gentleman named Harry Fox was given the task of licensing recordings, collecting mechanical royalties, and then distributing those royalties to the appropriate publishers—along with continuing the other services the NMPA had already instituted.

When Harry Fox died in 1969, the Harry Fox Agency was created as a wholly owned subsidiary of the National Music Publishers' Association. Today the Harry Fox Agency no longer issues synchronization licenses, but it continues to issue mechanical licenses, as well as licenses for digital downloads, ringtones, and other new media.

The Harry Fox Agency is also involved in other facets of music publishing, including foreign administration (see chapter nine). More information on the Harry Fox Agency is available by going to harryfox.com or by writing to The Harry Fox Agency, 711 Third Ave., New York, NY, 10017. The phone number is (212) 370-5330; and the fax number is (646) 487-6779.

good track record for making proper payments, and since her new album is another super seller, Sam's Smalltime Music Publishing Company is soon reaping the profits produced by the inclusion of the song from Sam's publishing catalog.

Whether Sam's song would have been on the album even if he had refused to grant a three-quarter rate is something he may never know. If Ed Promo knew that the song would be on the album whether or not Sam granted the rate, he's not likely to tell Sam. That would only encourage Sam to refuse to grant a reduced rate to Ed in the future.

Besides, the music industry—despite the fact that its actions are felt around the world via hit songs—is a very small community. Experienced executives in the music business know that making enemies is never a good idea. A year from now, Sam may be in a powerful position, and Ed Promo might be looking for a job. If Sam knows that Ed once took advantage of him, Ed isn't likely to find employment at Sam's Bigtime Music Publishing Company.

Scenario Number Two

Harry Hunk is recording an album of rock and roll songs from the 1950s and 1960s. Don Dealer has a publishing catalog consisting of songs that were hits during that era. As it turns out, three of the songs on Harry's album are published by Don Dealer's publishing company.

Record company executive Rita Rategetter calls Don to give him the good news and to ask for reduced rates on the three tunes. Don has been making deals for a long time. He would prefer not to give reduced rates if he doesn't have to, but Rita has done favors for him in the past, so he agrees to grant a three-quarter rate on all three songs on a "most favored nations" basis. In other words, if all of the other publishers whose songs appear on Harry's album grant reduced rates, Don will too. But, if anyone gets a higher rate, so does Don.

"However," Don tells Rita, "you have to agree that one of my songs will be released as a single, and that the mechanical royalties from any singles will be paid at the statutory rate."

Rita agrees to Don's request, which means Don's publishing company will receive mechanical royalties not only on album sales, but also on at least one single released from the album.

Let's say Harry Hunk's album sells 500,000 units. Since there are three songs on the album published by Don Dealer, Don's publishing company gets 6.825 cents (75 percent of 9.1 cents) times 500,000 for each song. Don's company has grossed $102,375.

However, since Rita agreed to release one of Don's songs as one of Harry's singles in exchange for receiving the reduced rate on the album, there are more mechanical royalties for Don to earn—this time at 9.1 cents per unit. If the single sells 100,000 units, that's another $9,100 in mechanical income for Don Dealer. And, if either of his other songs is released as a single, that's even more mechanical royalty income at the statutory rate.

Scenario Number Three

Reissue Records is putting out a compilation album of Christmas songs at a budget retail price. Fred Fooz from the label contacts the publishers of twenty different Christmas songs, offering an advance payment on 50,000 units in return for a three-quarter rate. In other words, Fred offers to pay each of the publishers—in advance of the album's release—three-quarters of the current statutory mechanical rate times 50,000. In exchange for receiving the advance money, the publishing company would have to accept a three-quarter rate on all units sold, even if the CD goes multiplatinum.

Xmas Xongs Publishing owns the song "Santa's Supercharged Sleigh." When the licensing person at Xmas Xongs gets Fred Fooz's request, she has to ask herself a couple of questions.

1. Is it likely the album will sell more than 37,500 units? 37,500 is 75 percent of 50,000. If the album sells 37,499 copies or less, Xmas Xongs Publishing technically will have been paid more than the statutory rate (or stat rate) on units sold. If the sales reach 37,501 units, Xmas Xongs will be receiving less than statutory. If the sales figures reach 50,000, the publisher will

hit the 75-percent-of-stat mark. (And, of course, from 50,000 units sold on up, the rate will continue to be 75 percent.)

2. If she turns down the request for the reduced rate, will the song be excluded from the album? After all, the record label has contacted twenty different publishers. If only fifteen songs end up on the album, Reissue Records's reduced rate request can be turned down by as many as five publishers and the label will still have fifteen songs at the three-quarter rate.

There is no way for the licensing person to know the answers to these questions. Her best courses of action are to either: (1) turn down the reduced rate request and keep her fingers crossed, or (2) agree to the rate on a "most favored nations" basis. By going with the latter choice, Xmas Xongs will either end up with an advance payment on 50,000 units or will be paid the statutory rate (if Reissue Records decides to include one or more songs on the album owned by publishers who decide not to agree to the rate).

Scenario Number Four

Linda Lucky has recently started a publishing company in New York City and has already had a couple of hits. Linda gets a license request from the Harry Fox Agency, informing her that a small record company in the Midwest has recorded one of her songs and wants a reduced rate.

Linda realizes that the chances of getting a hit on a small label with an unknown artist are very poor. Since there isn't much money to be made from this release, she decides to try to make as much as she can out of the situation and refuses to grant a reduced rate.

The Harry Fox Agency gives this information to the small record company's president, Sid Sneaky. Sid agrees to pay the statutory rate because he really wants to release the record. The Harry Fox Agency issues a statutory mechanical license to Sid's record company. As it turns out, the record becomes a regional hit, selling 30,000 copies.

Several months pass, and Linda Lucky realizes that she hasn't received any mechanical royalties from Sid Sneaky. Since Sid's company is over a thousand miles away, it's not feasible for Linda to send her accountant to the Midwest to audit Sid's company, especially since the record didn't sell enough copies to become a national hit.

As luck would have it, several publishers have been complaining to the Harry Fox Agency about lack of payments from Sid Sneaky, so HFA sends an auditor to Sid's company and discovers that he owes tens of thousands of dollars to a host of music publishers. Soon Linda Lucky and the other publishers receive their royalties, thanks to the Fox Agency's efforts.

As strange as some of these scenarios may seem, they represent everyday life in the music business. Understandably, most record companies want to pay as little as they can for the use of songs, and most publishers want to make as much money as possible every time one of their songs is used. It is this ongoing, back-and-forth action between licensors and licensees that helps to make the music industry an interesting place to work, even for those who aren't songwriters or performers.

Sampling

Sampling is when an artist uses a piece of a pre-existing recording (or *sample*) in a new recording. For example, a while back, Warren G and Nate Dogg had a chart-topping hit with a song called

"Regulate," which sampled a song from my publishing catalog. The recording consisted of Warren G and Nate Dogg doing a medium-tempo "singing rap" (for lack of a better description) over the keyboard portion of Michael McDonald's recording of "I Keep Forgettin'." In other words, although the lyrics and tune of "Regulate" were written by Warren G, a good portion of the actual recording used to make the recording entitled "Regulate" was, in fact, the original recording of Michael McDonald's keyboard performance from his recording of "I Keep Forgettin'."

In some situations, a sample might consist of no more than a portion of the bass line of a pre-existing recording. In others, an entire pre-existing master might be used, with additional lyrics and/or instrumentation added to it. Or, the whole chorus of a pre-existing recording might be stripped into a new recording.

The above described examples of samples would be, in most cases, defined as "derivative works" (which finally leads us to what all of this sampling stuff has to do with mechanical royalties in the first place).

Since you now know that the right "to prepare derivative works based upon the copyrighted work" is one of the six exclusive rights of the copyright owner (remember "Yo! Mary Had a Miniature Infant Sheep"?), then you know that if someone else wishes to create a new work based upon your copyrighted work, they she must secure the right to do so from you as the owner of the pre-existing copyrighted work.

> In the music industry, record companies are usually allowed forty-five days after the end of each quarter to make royalty payments.

How much a music publisher decides to charge for that right (should the publisher decide to grant the right at all) is variable, and is generally based on the extent of the sample in question. For instance, if only the bass, rhythm guitar, and drum pattern of a pre-existing recording are used by an artist who then creates new lyrics, a new chorus, new background vocals, and new horn parts, the publisher of the pre-existing song might determine that she should receive 50 percent of the mechanical royalties derived from the new work.

If more of the song is used, the publisher might ask for 75 percent of the mechanical royalties; conversely, if less is used, the percentage could drop considerably. If only a small fraction of the song is used, the publisher might agree to a *buy-out* (or one-time fee), granting the use of the sample without requiring the sampler to pay any future mechanical royalties at all.

The whole area of "sampling" can frequently be a one-sided negotiation. Whether the publisher charges a high percentage, a low percentage, or a small "buy-out" fee, the amount charged is up to the publisher of that pre-existing work since any use of the copyright without the permission of the copyright owner is, of course, an infringement.

I have had numerous situations where I or one of my co-publishers has determined that the new lyrics of a derivative work which sampled one of our copyrights was so extremely offensive, we simply turned down the request altogether (or at least asked that the lyrics be rewritten). For those about to cry "censorship," I can only point out that one such request on my part for an extreme lyric "cleanup" resulted in a gold single and a multi-platinum album. In its original form, the derivative work would have received no airplay at all (or would have been so full of bleeps and edits as to be practically impossible to listen to).

Sometimes a derivative work contains so much of a pre-existing work that the publisher of the pre-existing work can demand ownership or co-ownership of the new work, rather than just a share in the mechanical royalties and other income derived from the new work. I've demanded copyright ownership on plenty of occasions, when so much of one of my songs was used, it would have been ridiculous not to require that I own, or at least co-own, the copyright in the derivative work.

In other situations, however, ownership of copyright in a derivative work can be troublesome. It's times like this that copyright ownership can get a bit tricky.

Why? Because those of us who receive a lot of sample requests have discovered that there frequently can be additional *uncleared* samples (i.e., samples for which the artist did not get permission) in the same song in which our pre-existing copyright is sampled. If I claim copyright co-ownership of such a derivative work, and if the owner of the uncleared sample decides to sue for copyright infringement, then my company gets sued too, because I am one of the owners of the new work in question.

Therefore, in many situations that I'm familiar with, although the publisher of a pre-existing work continues to own that pre-existing work in its original form, that publisher will enter into an agreement with the "sampler" which grants the "pre-existing work" publisher an *"income interest participation"* in the new work, rather than actual copyright ownership of that work.

Are there exceptions? Sure there are. It's the music business. I've demanded copyright ownership on plenty of occasions when so much of one of my songs was used that it would seem ridiculous not to require that I own, or at least co-own, the copyright in the derivative work. In other situations, however, I've taken the safer approach, which is to require an income interest participation in the mechanical royalties, as well as in the other types of royalties described in this chapter.

To be thorough, I should point out that the creator of the derivative work (the sampler) not only has to get permission from the owner of the sampled song, but from the owner of the pre-existing master recording as well.

❧ SEVEN ❧

Synchronization Royalties

Synchronization royalties are monies earned by publishers for granting the right to use a song in a film or television show. (Synchronization royalties are also earned on commercials and via some new technology. See the discussion of commercial royalties on page 64 and of new technology royalties on page 78.) The word *synchronization* generally refers to when a song appears *in synch* with the visual images on the screen.

A synchronization license gives a film or television show the right to use a song. Unlike mechanical royalties, there isn't a compulsory synchronization rate. When it comes to determining how much to charge for the use of a song in a movie or television show, it's every publisher for himself.

Negotiating *synch fees*, as they are called in the business, is an art form unto itself that—depending on the skill of the negotiator—can mean a difference of thousands of dollars to the publisher (and, of course, to the songwriter whose publisher is doing the negotiating). Payment for the use of a song in a film can be either very small (for a low-budget film) or up to hundreds of thousands of dollars (for a big-budget film that uses a song as well as the song's title as the title of the movie).

Among the variables that can determine how much a publisher requests for a synch license are: the film's budget; the length of the use; whether the song is featured or is simply background music; the number of times the song is used in the film; whether the song is used over the opening or closing credits; and so on.

Once a publisher has been made aware that a film company wants to use one of his songs in a motion picture, the same strategy applies as in negotiating reduced mechanical rates: the film company wants to pay as little as possible, and the publisher wants to get as much as possible.

In many cases, film and television producers rely on music clearance organizations to handle the negotiation procedure for them.

Unfortunately for the publisher, many film companies (or their appointed clearance organizations) begin the synch license negotiation process long before a film is completed (sometimes even before a film is started), so any song can be dropped and replaced with another number from a publisher more willing to negotiate on the film company's terms.

The other terms of a synchronization license differ from company to company. Usually the license will require that the royalty amount be paid within a certain amount of time (such as within thirty days; prior to the release of the film; or before the first airing of the television show or commercial).

REAL-LIFE SCENARIO NUMBER ONE

I was once contacted by a film company that wanted to use a song published by a firm I worked for. I was told that they might want to use the song both in the film and as the title, and that they were willing to pay a fee that would be higher than for a standard film use, but not nearly as high as what I might usually charge for a title, just in case they decided to go with another title.

One phone call to a friend of mine who had worked on the film got me all of the information I needed. The movie was already finished; the song in question was already the title of the film; the song was used over the closing credits; and the melody of the song appeared in the score throughout the picture. For the film company there was no turning back without spending an absolute fortune. Needless to say, I quoted a high fee and ignored the film company's complaints about my lack of fairness.

Was acquiring this inside information "cheating" on my part? Not really. After all, the film company was trying to mislead me by implying that a high fee could mean a loss of the song in the movie. "All is fair in love, war, and the music business."

REAL-LIFE SCENARIO NUMBER TWO

Synch fees for the use of a song in a documentary are generally much lower than those for feature films. Budgets for documentaries are usually quite low, as are the profits. This being the case, many music publishers grant synch licenses for documentaries for just a few thousand dollars—sometimes for just a few hundred dollars.

A few years ago, I had just finished negotiating a $25,000 synch fee for the use of two songs in a documentary when I received a call requesting the use of two songs for $4,000 each in another documentary. I knew two things about this second documentary: that its budget was at least as large as the documentary I had just charged $25,000, and that it had a good chance of doing extremely well at the box office. On top of everything else, one of the two songs requested was a song I had just gotten $12,500 for in the first documentary.

Having done so well on documentary number one, I refused to grant synch licenses for the two songs in the second documentary for less than $10,000 each. To my surprise, the film company passed. The one thing I hadn't taken into account was that the second documentary wasn't finished yet.

Several months later, the second documentary was released without the two songs from my publishing company. To make matters worse, the documentary's soundtrack album sold three million copies. If I had agreed to the original fee request of $8,000 for the two songs, and if both songs had appeared on the soundtrack album, I would have made much more in mechanical royalties than the $20,000 I was demanding for synch royalties.

I made this particular blunder several years ago, when the statutory mechanical rate was 5.25 cents. Two songs at 5.25 cents each times three million comes to $315,000. Add the original synch license request of $8,000 for the two songs, and you'll see that I blew a possible gross of $323,000—all because I made the mistake of comparing one documentary deal with another,

Music Clearance Organizations

Music clearance organizations act as negotiators on behalf of parties wishing to use copyrighted music—mainly in the area of movies and television shows. Arlene Fishbach heads her own extremely successful clearance organization, Arlene Fishbach Enterprises, which is based in Los Angeles. Arlene states the clearance organization's foremost activity: "Our primary function is to clear music—to act as an agent for the producer of a film or television project—by negotiating synch fees and the rights acquired by payment of those fees so that nothing can stand in the way of the release of that project."

Fishbach explains how this process typically works: "A producer will call us and say he's working on a project; he then tells us what it's all about. This includes a synopsis of the project, who's in it, where he's intending to distribute it once it's completed, and where he may plan on distributing it three or five years from now. Then we discuss what kind of music he wants.

"Sometimes he already has a specific idea of what songs he wants to use, sometimes he doesn't. Depending on how specific he is, we either recommend songs to him or we make preliminary plans to clear the songs he wants by discussing with him exactly what rights he needs.

"Usually what we will do is determine the best possible 'rights package' for him so that if, in a year or eighteen months from now, he decides he wants to distribute the product to the home video market, those rights will have already been negotiated for him. This way the publisher cannot say eighteen months later, 'Okay, this is a really successful film; therefore, I want ten million dollars for my song to be used in the home video release.' Everything is negotiated up front in an effort to protect the producer and the distributor."

Why would a producer pay a music clearance agency to handle such negotiations rather than go directly to the specific publishers who control the songs he wants to use? Actually, some producers do go straight to the source. For those who prefer to handle their own negotiations with publishers, clearance agencies can still perform a vital function. "For many clients, all we do is research," Fishbach says. "We'll supply them the publishing companies' names and the contacts, so they can call themselves if they choose."

Fishbach points out that those personal contacts are a valuable asset for clearing houses. "This is a business that's based on relationships. A clearance organization that deals with the same publishers day in and day out usually can get faster and more thorough responses than an individual who doesn't know the major players in the publishing business."

unrelated, documentary deal. If you consider the fact that both songs could have been released as singles, the number goes even higher. All is fair. . . .

COMMERCIAL ROYALTIES

There are several different types of synchronization licenses. Along with synch licenses for movies and television shows, there are synch licenses for commercials, promotional videos, nontheatrical in-house meetings, pay/cable/subscription television (as opposed to "free" television), and a variety of other specific uses.

In recent years, the income that can be made from the use of a song in a commercial has increased substantially. The use of R&B, rap, hip-hop, rock and roll, country, and other popular song genres in advertising campaigns has become more and more commonplace. Some publishers have demanded (and gotten) more than a million dollars for the use of a current hit or rock and roll standard to advertise beer, soft drinks, credit cards, computers, and other items. (A million dollars is obviously at the extremely high end of the synch fee spectrum, but this fee has been paid on many occasions.)

In most cases, a publisher is contacted about synch fees by an advertising agency representing a particular product. Usually the agency asks for a one-year license with an option to extend that term if the campaign is successful. The amount of money a publisher can get for such a use depends primarily on the budget for the commercial. The bigger the budget, the higher the synch fee is likely to be.

There is usually a lot of guesswork involved in negotiations over commercial synch fees. No doubt, many publishers have asked for a fee much lower than the advertising agency might have been willing to pay. Some parameters that publishers consider when setting a synch fee are: (1) the territory involved; (2) the duration (or term) of the license; (3) the length of the commercial; (4) the importance of the song being licensed; (5) whether the commercial will be used on radio, on television, or both; (6) whether the commercial will be used on the Internet; (7) whether there will be a parody lyric involved; and (8) whether the advertiser requests an exclusive use. Let's consider these factors individually.

1. The commercial territory. Some commercials are national, some are local, and others fall into some sort of middle ground. A commercial advertising a product such as laundry detergent is usually of the national variety. In other words, it appears all over the country during a commercial break in a network show. A commercial advertising a small clothing store in your neighborhood is a local commercial that is seen only in your viewing area. Commercials that can fall somewhere in-between a national and a local advertisement are those that appear only in specific regions. If an auto parts store has branches only in St. Louis, Chicago, and Miami, then those are the only regions in which the commercial will air. There are also commercials—known as spot advertisements—that showcase a national product, but only in specific regions at specific times.

Therefore, the territory of a commercial can demand any number of variations regarding the fee that might be asked by the publisher.

A national commercial will bring thousands of dollars more than a local commercial, whereas commercials that are shown in only three or four major cities will usually fall somewhere in-between.

2. The commercial term. The duration of a commercial use can be anywhere from very brief (sometimes only a day or a week) to interminable. Once again, the synch fee involved can be very small for a short campaign or well over a million dollars for a multiyear use.

If an ad agency requests the use of a song for a year with an option to use it for a second year, it is common practice among publishers to grant the option request, provided that the advertiser agrees to pay a synch fee that is anywhere from 10 to 20 percent higher for the second year.

In other words, if a dog food company wants to use "I Love My Dog" for one year with a one-year option, the publisher of "I Love My Dog" might agree to a fee of $250,000 for one year with a 15 percent increase for the second year. If the commercial causes the dog food company to sell a lot of dog food, the company will probably want to use the song for a second year.

Under the license agreement the dog food company has with the publisher, upon picking up the option for the second year, the dog food company will owe the publisher $287,500 (or $250,000 plus 15 percent of $250,000). So, for the two years combined, the publisher has grossed $537,500. Of course, since the second year is an option, if the dog food company decides not to use the song after the end of the first year, no further synch royalties are due to the publisher.

The variations on the commercial term are numerous. I have been involved with one song that was used to advertise a particular product for nine years and ended up generating millions of dollars. I'm sure there are others that have been used even longer.

3. The commercial length. The length of a commercial can be as short as ten seconds or as long as a minute and a half. In special situations (such as when a national soft drink is introducing a superstar as a new spokesperson), the length of a commercial can be even longer. A publisher will be inclined to ask more for a commercial that is sixty seconds long than for one that is thirty seconds long.

4. The importance of the song. This is a factor that can make a difference of thousands of dollars in the publisher's asking price. Although it should be obvious, the importance of a song can sometimes be overlooked, especially by a major publisher dealing with thousands of copyrights.

Determining the importance of a song is, in some ways, a subjective process. However, it should be obvious that a song that has become a standard—via multiple recordings and continued popularity over a long period of time—is more important than a song that was once a minor hit. Some publishers consider certain songs to be of too much historical and/or social importance to allow any advertiser to use them. Others consider a song too important only until someone offers an amount of money large enough to change their minds.

There is also the question of the importance of the song to the advertiser. If a particular song is obviously the perfect choice for a product, a publisher will probably be able to charge more to that advertiser than to another who simply happened to like the song's melody.

Many songwriters have clauses in their publishing agreements that allow them the final decision about whether their songs will be used to advertise a product or service. These clauses may also give the songwriter final say over the manner in which the song will be used in the advertisement.

5. The commercial medium (radio, television, or both). To refer to the use of a song on a radio commercial as a synch use is technically incorrect, since there is nothing to synchronize the music with. However, since many advertisers sometimes use the same audio track for a radio commercial as for the television commercial, the term *synch license* or *commercial synch license* is usually used even to denote a license for a commercial used only on radio.

If an advertiser wants to use a song in both television and radio commercials, the publisher will almost always ask more than she would ask for a commercial used just on television. Under similar circumstances, advertisers usually expect to pay less for a song used only on a radio commercial than for the same song used only on a television commercial.

6. Commercials on the Internet. If the advertiser plans to show its commercial on the Internet, whether on the product's own Web site or on other parties' Web sites, the publisher usually charges an additional fee. Some publishers feel the Internet fee should be substantial because once the commercial is up on the Internet, it can be viewed by anyone anywhere in the world— even if the television version of the commercial airs only in the state of Kansas.

7. Parody lyrics. Here's another word publishers sometimes use improperly. The word *parody* actually means a humorous or farcical recasting of a literary or musical work. (Previously, we discussed how the Supreme Court has developed its own definition of *parody*, which would appear to be rather broad.) In the music publishing business, the term *parody* can also apply to lyrics that have been changed to advertise a product. All of us have seen commercials on television in which the melody of a familiar song has been used in conjunction with lyrics that promote a particular product.

When a copyrighted song is used in a commercial, performance royalties are paid by the performing rights society with which the song's publisher and songwriter are affiliated. Some performing rights societies pay less for the performance of a song if a parody lyric has been used instead of the original lyrics. (Don't ask me why. It's just one of the mysteries of the music business.) Therefore, some publishers will charge more for the use of a song if the advertiser insists on changing the lyrics, because the performance royalty income will be less.

In many cases, a songwriter's contract with a publisher will include a clause that gives the songwriter the final say in any lyric changes of this type.

8. Exclusive use. In the advertising business, there are several types of exclusive uses. The most common is referred to as *"exclusive to product."* For instance, if the dog food company mentioned earlier wants to use "I Love My Dog," they will ask that they have the exclusive use of the song for pet food commercials for the duration of the commercial term. If the ASPCA wanted to use the same song to advertise the importance of being kind to animals, the publisher would be able to allow that use because it doesn't conflict with the dog food company's use.

Another type of exclusive use is by territory. If the dog food company advertises and sells its dog food only in California, it might ask for product exclusivity for the state of California. The publisher can then allow another dog food company that advertises and sells its product only in New York to use the same song. However, the publisher has to be cautious in granting product exclusivity for just one state or a small group of states. If a national dog food company wants to use "I Love My Dog" for a commercial that would cover the entire U.S., and the publisher has already granted an *exclusive to product* license for "I Love My Dog" to a dog food company in California, then the national dog food company is going to start looking for another song. It's up to the publisher to decide whether the use in California is worth the gamble of possibly blowing a national use.

Sometimes the situation can be even more complicated; there are occasions when an adver-

Randy's Thoughts on the Use of Hit Songs in Commercials

There have been loud complaints by some prominent rock stars in the last few years regarding the use of hit songs in commercials. Their arguments are usually based on the fact that these songs are of historical significance; that they are pieces of art being wrongfully used to sell soap, soft drinks, and other products; or that, by allowing a song to be used in such a manner, the song's creator is "selling out." (That's a term we used in the 1960s.)

In many ways I can see their point. How can a particular superstar possibly need any more money? Does she really have to turn one of her biggest hits into a sixty-second commercial for Pepsi or Coke? Surely, the only reason an artist would possibly do such a thing is that she is being paid in the millions of dollars. It can't be solely because she believes in the product. Otherwise, why not just make the commercial for free?

I used to have the same attitude: No rock and roll standard should be used in a commercial. However, I've since learned that many of those songs were written by songwriters who aren't superstars. A few years ago I was involved in licensing a song that you have probably heard hundreds of times. Before I started making commercial deals using the song, it had been earning the writer a few hundred dollars a year in performance income because it still got a lot of airplay on radio stations that played oldies.

In a matter of months, I issued two commercial synch licenses—totaling over one hundred-thousand dollars—for the song. It was the most money that songwriter had ever seen at one time, and he was extremely grateful. Of course I won't embarrass him by mentioning his name, but he was over seventy years old when I made the deals. His share added a nice bonus to his retirement fund. He even spent some of it to go into the studio and make more demos!

So, I have—to some extent—changed my mind about the use of hit songs in commercials. The superstars who turn their hits into jingles may be suffering from some serious greed, but that elderly gentleman who wrote the song I'm referring to finally made the kind of money he would have made a long time ago if the mechanical royalty rate had been higher and if other sources of income (such as the use of rock and roll songs in commercials) had been available to him back then.

tiser will ask for *total* exclusivity on a song. In this case, the publisher will usually ask for more money than he would in almost any other synch license situation. The reason the publisher can be expected to charge a large fee is because the advertiser is asking the publisher to give up the chance to allow any other advertisers of any type of product to use that particular song for the duration of the commercial term.

Granting total exclusivity on a song is almost always a roll of the dice for the publisher. Some songs just seem to lend themselves to commercials. In one of the publishing companies I managed, several songs generated calls almost every week. If I had decided to grant a total exclusive on one of those songs, I would have been passing up the opportunity to allow the same song to be used in other ad campaigns. Therefore, if an ad agency requests a total exclusivity license for a song, the publishing company's licensing department has to ask for an amount equal to or higher than the amount it estimates the song would have received if several *exclusive to product* uses had been granted.

✺ EIGHT ✺

Performance Royalties

As I said in chapter three, one of the six exclusive rights of the copyright owner is the right to perform (or authorize others to perform) the copyrighted work publicly. Beginning with ASCAP in 1914, and later with BMI and SESAC, there are three performing rights societies that make sure the copyright owners of songs are paid performance royalties when those songs are performed in public.

Each of these three societies issues licenses to those companies and establishments that publicly perform (or allow others to publicly perform) music as a part of their business operations: radio and television stations, restaurants, nightclubs, dance halls, Web sites, and other venues and broadcasters. The licenses require these music users to make payments to the performing rights society in return for the right to perform the songs licensed. Once a society determines the performance royalties owed to the publisher and songwriter of a song being performed, the society makes payments to the appropriate parties. For example, a performance of a song on a television show would lead to performance royalties being paid to the publisher and songwriter of that particular song by the performing rights society with which that publisher and writer are affiliated.

The societies do the legwork required to make sure songwriters and music publishers are properly compensated for public performances, since it would be impossible for the individual writers and publishers to keep track of every time their songs are performed. Of course, it's also impossible for the societies to keep track of every performance, so each society has devised its own system to help it: (1) come as close as possible to making accurate assessments of performances, and (2) make payments to writers and publishers.

Before we begin to explore the three performing rights societies individually, there are several important pieces of information you should know, beginning with the relationship between the songwriter, the publisher, and the societies.

A writer can belong to only one society at a time, although co-writers of the same song can belong to different societies. In other words, Al might be a member of ASCAP, Bob might be affiliated with BMI, and Sally might belong to SESAC. If the three of them write a song together, each will be paid his or her share of performance royalties by the performing rights society to which he or she belongs.

The same is true for publishers. Al's publishing company must be a member of ASCAP; Bob's publisher must be with BMI; and Sally's publishing company must be affiliated with SESAC. Many publishing firms actually consist of several different publishing companies, each affiliated with one of the three societies.

Although a publishing company rarely changes its affiliation from one society to another (primarily because it would mean all of the writers signed to that publisher would have to be able and willing to change their affiliations simultaneously), many songwriters have been known to switch societies at some time in their careers. However, no songwriter or single publishing company can be affiliated with more than one society at a time.

It is also very important to note that the three U.S. performing rights societies license only something called *small rights*, or nondramatic performances—that is, performances of songs on radio, television, the Internet, in nightclubs, hotels, and so forth. *Grand rights*, which include the rights to perform songs in a Broadway show or any other dramatic context, are outside the realm of the performing rights societies. (See the discussion of royalties for grand rights on page 74.)

ASCAP

ASCAP stands for the American Society of Composers, Authors, and Publishers. (The term *author* as used in this context is synonymous with the word *lyricist*.) ASCAP was founded in New York City in 1914, making it the first performing rights society in the country.

ASCAP was created so that those performing music publicly would finally be forced to comply with the Copyright Act (which had added public performance to the list of the copyright owner's exclusive rights a few years earlier) and, of course, to pay the copyright owners royalties for those public performances.

ASCAP acquires monies to pay copyright owners by licensing (issuing a license and charging a fee to) users of music for public performance. Among the licensees who pay fees to ASCAP are: the major television networks, local and cable television, radio stations, public broadcasters, colleges and universities, restaurants, hotels, concert halls, Muzak, and other users. The licensing fees ASCAP charges vary depending on the size of the licensee and the amount of music generally used. A local television station will be charged a much lower fee than a network, while a small restaurant will pay less than a radio station in a major market.

Licensing fees for songs in the ASCAP repertoire are determined, in some cases, by negotiations with national organizations representing hotels, restaurants, radio stations, etc. And if a user feels a fee is too high, that user can ask a New York federal judge to determine a reasonable fee.

ASCAP can only issue licenses for songs in its repertoire, and cannot issue licenses for music in the public domain. (Users of music in the public domain do not need to negotiate a license with any of the rights societies.) Some music users—especially those who use a society's songs infrequently—may choose to negotiate directly with the copyright holder, even if the copyright holder is a member of ASCAP or another rights society. However, those who frequently have ASCAP songs being performed will almost always agree to pay the fee for ASCAP's blanket license, which gives the licensee the right to use any song that is in ASCAP's repertoire.

Television royalties are paid out on the basis of a census, or complete count, of all performances on network television (ABC, CBS, FOX, NBC, UPN, WB). In addition, ASCAP surveys millions of hours of local television broadcasts annually, creating a virtual census of syndicated series, feature films, movies of the week, etc.—performances that appear outside of network television.

Songwriter Marilyn Bergman, ASCAP President and Chairman of the Board since 1994, explains some of the reasons she's an ASCAP advocate:

> *ASCAP is a remarkable organization. It is, in fact, the premiere performing rights organization in the world. It is the most fair, the most dependable and the most protective of creators' rights. We pay royalties based on earnings and based on fairness. The most successful and the newest guy on the block get paid the same amount for comparable performance. And you can rely on ASCAP throughout your career—not just at a particular high point—as a steady, solid support.*
>
> *We are the only United States society that is owned by writers and publishers, and whose president is a writer. This structure uniquely equips us to best understand the needs of our 200,000 active composers, lyricists, and publisher members, unencumbered by any other interests.*
>
> *ASCAP is also the only United States society that conducts open membership meetings and issues complete financial reports to its members. We were the first society to offer our members important benefits, such as a credit union and instrument insurance; the first to establish an innovative system—ACE (ASCAP Clearance Express)—to make title, writer, and publisher information available through the Internet.*
>
> *ASCAP is also the acknowledged leader in revenue collections and royalty distributions, and in negotiating license fees with the users of music. ASCAP is committed to ensuring that our members receive the highest payment possible when their music is performed outside the United States. To that end, ASCAP has instituted technical visits to foreign societies to ensure proper identification and crediting of our members' performed works, and we have also welcomed their visits to ASCAP to learn more about our operations firsthand.*
>
> *Since 1914, ASCAP has aggressively championed creators' rights and continues to assume leadership in this area as our music enters cyberspace. In fact, we have a new-media license that is considered a model license in the digital world. And while we are busy making sure our members are getting paid for getting played, we continue to build new careers and catalogs via the workshops, showcases, and educational programs sponsored by the ASCAP Foundation.*
>
> *These are the reasons I am a member of ASCAP and why I choose to remain a member. In all ways I can think of, it pays to belong to ASCAP.*

BMI

Broadcast Music, Inc.—BMI—was formed in 1940, providing ASCAP with its first serious competition. Prior to the founding of BMI, songwriters and publishers of some types of music had been denied the right to share in performance royalty income. BMI President Emeritus Frances W. Preston explains: "In 1940 BMI initiated the 'Open Door Policy,' extending participation in performing rights income to all creators of all types of music, at a time when they were denied participation by other American performing rights societies. This policy helped facilitate the great explosion of American music that has continued throughout the history of BMI."

Whatever its reasons, ASCAP had chosen to deny membership to writers and publishers of R&B and country, as well as some other types of music. (To be fair, I should mention that today all three U.S. performing rights societies are open to all types of music.)

These broadcasters felt that the fees they were then being charged by ASCAP were too high. During 1940, BMI affiliated with many publishers and songwriters. ASCAP's contract with the broadcasters expired on December 31 of that year, and suddenly there were no ASCAP songs being broadcast. By airing only non-ASCAP songs on the radio, the broadcasters were attempting to avoid paying the fees ASCAP was demanding.

Meanwhile, the Justice Department filed civil suits alleging antitrust violations on the parts of ASCAP, BMI, NBC, and CBS. Consent decrees were eventually signed to settle these suits. ASCAP resolved its negotiations with the broadcasters, and soon the music of both societies was back on the airwaves.

Like ASCAP, BMI issues licenses to those who are involved in the public performance of music. BMI licenses television and radio stations, cable program services, radio and television networks, PBS, restaurants, nightclubs, Web sites, and many other users of music.

Frances Preston gives some of the reasons she considers BMI the best society for writers and publishers:

> *BMI is responsible for most innovations in the performing rights field, including being the first to distribute royalties for FM radio airplay and television background music, and now, the first to create a distinct and complete logging and distribution system for college radio airplay.*
>
> *We have always led the way in creating awards and recognition through the media for our songwriters and composers. We are proud of all the musical genres in our repertoire and all the creators of music who have entrusted us with their representation.*
>
> *BMI has always led the way in the fight to protect the rights of composers, songwriters, and copyright owners locally, nationally, and internationally. We also employ the most advanced technological systems of any performing rights organization in the world. Our staff prides itself on the quality of service we provide to the largest and most creative body of composers, songwriters, and publishers anywhere in the world.*

SESAC

Of the three performing rights societies, SESAC runs a distant third in size. The organization was formed by Paul Heinecke in 1930, at which time it was called the Society of European Stage Authors and Composers. (In its early days, SESAC primarily represented European works. Since this is no longer its main function, the society has reduced its name to simply SESAC.)

Although there are similarities between the functions of SESAC and the other two U.S. performing rights societies, SESAC is profoundly different because it is a privately owned company. SESAC's current owners are Freddie Gershon, Ira Smith, and Stephen Swid along with the merchant banking house of Allen & Company.

Whereas BMI and ASCAP operate on a not-for-profit basis and pay most of the money they collect to songwriters and publishers, SESAC pays out approximately half of its earnings to its affiliates, keeping the rest for company profits. SESAC's position is that, by applying a selective policy to the acquisition of repertoire, it can afford to maintain competitive payment to its writers and publishers.

Also, SESAC provides its members with personalized services not common to the other two societies, like catalog consulting, legal advice, and teaming up songwriters for collaboration purposes.

According to Pat Rogers, Senior Vice President of Corporate Relations and Artist Development:

> As the technological leader among the nation's performing rights organizations, SESAC was the first P.R.O. to employ state-of-the-art Broadcast Data Systems (BDS) performance detection. SESAC utilizes BDS in conjunction with cutting edge ConfirMedia Watermarking technology, providing SESAC's writer and publisher affiliates with the fastest, most accurate royalty payment available anywhere. The system to compute compensation is based on many factors, including music trade publication chart activity, broadcast logs, computer database information, and state-of-the-art monitoring.

Ellen Bligh Jones, SESAC's Senior Director of Corporate Relations, explains some of the organization's attributes for its members and licensees:

> If the phrase "quality vs. quantity" ever mattered, SESAC is the place. While SESAC is the smallest of the three U.S. performing rights organizations, the company believes its size is its largest advantage. SESAC prides itself in developing individual relationships with both songwriters and publishers.
>
> Licensees benefit from the intimate atmosphere, with a licensing staff dedicated to meeting the needs of music users quickly and satisfactorily. And because our repertory concerns itself only with quality copyrights, the music user doesn't have to sift through the millions of infrequently used copyrights common to other performing rights organizations to access the usable copyrights.

Like the other two societies, SESAC issues licenses to users of music for public performance and has reciprocal arrangements with foreign societies. In fact, SESAC was the first U.S. performing rights organization to establish relations with China, having executed a reciprocal agreement in May of 1996.

Royalties for Grand Rights

Grand rights—also known as *dramatic performance rights*—are the rights granted to publicly perform musical compositions in a dramatic setting (plays, ballets, Broadway shows, and so on). As you have already learned, the three performing rights societies are generally limited to licensing small rights (nondramatic rights) and wouldn't be involved in negotiating grand rights.

A theater group that is planning to perform a musical on Broadway would have to negotiate and pay dramatic performance rights royalties to the copyright owner of the compositions in that musical. Because dramatic performance rights are so uniquely different from some of the other types of rights we have discussed, the rules governing their administration sometimes differ as well.

Often, songwriters who write specifically for the theater reserve to themselves the right to license grand rights. Even writers who don't compose for the theater sometimes reserve the right to license grand rights, just in case one of their songs is chosen to be included in a musical or other dramatic setting. Therefore, although the publisher of a musical might control other types of rights for the individual songs from that musical (synch rights, mechanical licenses, print deals, etc.), grand rights would be controlled by the *writers* of that musical.

THE IMAGINARY MUSICAL SCENARIO

Roger Dietz and Murray Heart have written a musical entitled *Paint Your Trailer*. For the sake of this scenario, let's say that Dietz and Heart are signed to Sam's Bigtime Publishing Company, but that the control of the dramatic rights remains with Dietz and Heart. Therefore, if the Raving Lunatics Repertory Company wishes to put on a production of *Paint Your Trailer* at a particular venue, they must negotiate the grand rights royalty fees with Dietz and Heart.

Dietz and Heart have granted Sam's Bigtime Publishing Company the right to negotiate and issue licenses for other types of royalties (synch licenses, for instance). One of the twelve songs in *Paint Your Trailer* is called "Sodas, Sodas, Sodas." When a major soft drink company decided that "Sodas, Sodas, Sodas" would be the perfect song to use in its next ad campaign, the commercial synch license had to be negotiated with (and issued by) Sam's Bigtime Publishing Company.

The royalties from the Raving Lunatics Repertory Company were paid directly to Dietz and Heart. On the other hand, the synch royalties for the soft drink commercial were paid to Sam's Bigtime Publishing Company, which in turn paid Dietz and Heart their shares when the song-writers' next royalty statements were due.

Now let's say that Dietz and Heart are affiliated with BMI. We already know that, in this case, grand rights are the domain of the two writers. However, the musical is a big success, and another song from the show, "They Call the Breeze Belinda," becomes a hit record by Tony Bendit. The mechanical license is issued to Mr. Bendit's record company by either Sam's Bigtime Publishing Company or the Harry Fox Agency. When Sam receives mechanical royalties, he keeps his share and pays the writers their shares. And when the recording of "They Call the Breeze Belinda" is played on the radio, or when the song is performed by Tony on a late-night talk show, those performances fall into the category of nondramatic rights. BMI would then pay Sam's Bigtime Publishing Company the publisher's share of small performance rights royalties, and Dietz and Heart the songwriter's share of small performance rights royalties.

The Grand Rights Exception

Not every musical that appears on the stage is made up of a group of songs written by a writer specifically for that musical. There have been several theatrical shows that have consisted of songs written by various songwriters during a particular era. A musical about the early days of rock and roll, for instance, might consist of fifteen or twenty rock and roll hits from the late 1950s. Obviously, the writers of those songs had no way of knowing that their songs would eventually become part of a popular musical fifty years later. Therefore, it is unlikely that the songwriters reserved grand rights for themselves in their publisher contracts. And the publishers would have had no reason to consider granting such rights, since the songs weren't written specifically for a musical in the first place (as the aforementioned Dietz and Heart songs obviously were). In this case, the publishers (as opposed to the songwriters) would be in a position to grant grand rights to the party wishing to put on the musical in question. Grand rights royalties would then be paid to the publishers, who would each pay their writers the individual songwriters' shares.

THE REAL-LIFE MUSICAL SCENARIO

When I wrote the first edition of this book, there were no plans in the works for what is now affectionately referred to around my office as "the longest-running musical revue in Broadway history," *Smokey Joe's Cafe: The Songs of Leiber & Stoller*. As it turns out, *Smokey Joe's* just happens to fall into the category described above. That is, the show consists of almost forty songs written by Jerry Leiber and Mike Stoller over the course of several decades, beginning back in 1952.

Luckily, in this particular case, the songwriters happen to also be the publishers of most of the songs that appear in the show. However, the rights to those songs owned by outside publishers had to be negotiated between those outside publishers and the company that produced the musical. Furthermore, there were some songs used in *Smokey Joe's* for which a few subpublishers controlled the rights in their particular territories. Therefore, before the show could be performed overseas, the producers had to negotiate with those subpublishers to have the right to perform some of the show's songs in the particular territories those subpublishers control.

Having now gone through this process, I would strongly recommend that young songwriters do their best to specifically exclude grand rights from their songwriter agreements. The phenomenal success of *Smokey Joe's Cafe: The Songs of Leiber & Stoller* is solid evidence that you never know when your songs might be used in the context of a theatrical production.

⁘ NINE ⁘

Other Royalties

Print Royalties

Print royalties are monies earned from the sale of printed editions of songs. As I said in chapter one, this was the original source of income for music publishers and songwriters when music publishing was in its infancy in this country. Although print royalties have generally taken a back seat to mechanical, synchronization, and performance income, the printed editions of songs are still an important part of music publishing today.

Print royalties differ from other types of publishing income because printed music is not handled by all publishing companies in the same manner. For instance, some music publishers are large enough that they still print sheet music, folios, orchestral arrangements, and other print editions with their own facilities. Other publishers rely on companies known as print publishers to print music for them. Since so few music publishers are still in the market of printing their own music, let's turn our attention to the print publisher.

Print publishers are a very competitive breed. Their survival usually depends on acquiring the rights to create printed editions of hit songs. Because of this, print publishers attempt to make exclusive deals with copyright-owning publishers. These exclusive deals give the print publisher the right to create printed editions of all of the songs in the copyright-owning publisher's catalog for a particular length of time. One print publisher might own the print rights of a large number of copyright-owning publishers at one time.

The rights the print publisher acquires (depending on the parameters of the agreement) can include the rights to print sheet music (as well as to sell it in downloadable form over the Internet), to print folios, and to print arrangements for choruses, bands, and orchestras. In exchange for these rights, the print publisher usually pays an advance to the copyright-owning publisher, followed by a percentage of the royalties the print publisher earns from sales of the printed editions.

Of these various printed editions, sheet music is probably the most frequently published. Surprisingly, not all hit songs are considered marketable as sheet music. Due to the high costs of printing, print publishers tend to print only those songs that either make it to the very top of the charts or become standards over a period of time. Unlike the majority of the record-buying public, sheet music purchasers are usually musicians who want to learn how to play the song in question. Although a dance record with two chords and one lyrical phrase repeated over and over may become a big hit on the radio and among record buyers, sheet music sales would probably be minimal. A simple dance tune might come and go without ever being printed as sheet music.

A visit to the sheet music section of your local music store can be a very enlightening experience. What you will usually find in the racks are several current hits and dozens of standards from all eras. These standards will usually include pop ballads, gospel songs, songs frequently used at weddings, and the songs you hear performed by lounge acts around the globe.

Another type of printed edition is the folio. Folios are better known as songbooks to you and me. These folios come in a variety of styles, including *mixed, matching,* and *personality.* A mixed folio consists of a grab bag of songs that have something in common. Songbooks of heavy metal from the 1970s, favorite movie themes, and classic country songs would all be examples of mixed folios.

It is also common for a print publisher to release a folio that contains all of the songs from a hit album. Often this type of matching folio will have the same cover as the album in question. Another example of a matching folio would be one that comprises all of the songs used in a Broadway show.

Personality folios feature songs that are all related to a specific person, but they differ from matching folios because the personality may be a nonperforming songwriter or songwriting team, or the folio may contain hits from various albums by the same artist.

Those of us who have played in the school marching band or have sung in a choir are familiar with the many different types of arrangements available in printed editions. There are also folios and sheet music for easy piano, organ, guitar, and all other popular instruments.

New Technology Royalties

"New technology" is a sort of catch-all phrase for the royalty-earning areas that have come into existence over the last few years. In the music publishing business, we sometimes find ourselves creating terms for new royalty streams. When we talk about new technology, we generally mean digital downloads and other computer-related methods of earning (or at least trying to earn) royalties. We also use the phrase "new media" from time to time.

For instance, karaoke used to be in the category known as new media. Karaoke is now such a commonplace thing that people in the publishing business know exactly what it is and how to license it. But there was a time, in the early days of this new format, when publishers were all trying to determine how to license it. Why was karaoke difficult to get a handle on when it first came on the scene? Because it's a unique combination of mechanical, synch, and print. It took a little while for publishers to figure out what kind of fee to charge the manufacturers, and to create a new license specific to karaoke.

Remember when the singing fish first appeared? Several years ago, somebody came up with the idea of creating a rubber fish that looked like a real bass, stuffed and mounted. But, when its sensor was activated, the fish would start singing. Its mouth moved and its tail wagged back and forth. Some publishers considered it nothing more than a mechanical device, so they chose to charge the current statutory mechanical rate. But other publishers thought, *Wait, it's moving in synch with the music.* So, some of us lucky enough to have a song used in the singing fish created a new license that encompassed both synch and mechanical.

And then there's the Internet. Nothing has ever come along that has caused so much concern for copyright owners as the ability to illegally download copyrighted works. With the creation of file-sharing software and compressed music files, computer users suddenly found themselves able to download copyrighted works from the Internet for free. The major record labels were caught off guard by this new technology—a clear sign that the labels were behind the times.

A host of companies (Napster being the most famous in the early days) created services that allowed computer users to download practically any recording they could think of. Of course, as you learned in chapter two, the copyright owners of those songs and recordings have the right to be compensated for their use. When Napster and others devised ways for copyrighted works to be downloaded for free, the record labels, artists, music publishers, and songwriters all suffered great financial losses. Although a few companies came along that charged fees for downloading recordings and made proper payments to the copyright owners, they were vastly outnumbered by the illegal services.

Many class action lawsuits were filed not only by record labels and music publishers, but also by motion picture companies (since movies are also downloadable). The Recording Industry Association of America (RIAA) even began suing individuals who were downloading large numbers of recordings.

In 2001, Apple Computer, Inc. developed iTunes, which is both a program for downloading songs (onto Apple's iPod) and an Internet storefront for those songs. iTunes and similar music download services make sure that record labels and music publishers actually get paid for the millions of downloads that have taken place over the last few years. (By the way, Napster has now gone legit, properly paying for downloads of copyrighted works.)

The Harry Fox Agency issues licenses for downloads at the equivalent of the current statutory mechanical rate. The license issued by HFA is called a DPD, which stands for *digital phonorecord delivery.*

New technology is coming fast and furiously, and music publishers (as well as other copyright owners) are desperately trying to keep up with it all. Most publishers have found ways to deal with much of the new technology that now exists. Others are hanging on by the seat of their pants. The important thing to keep in mind is that all of these new technologies mean new sources of income for the music publisher and the songwriter.

All of the types of royalties we have covered are available to songwriters and music publishers because of the U.S. Copyright Act. The exclusive rights discussed in chapter three provide the copyright owner the right to receive mechanical, synchronization, performance, print, and new technology royalties. In this chapter, you will see that there is protection for songs in most territories outside of the United States as well, thanks to international copyright laws.

Royalties From Foreign Sources

It has been said that the popular songs created in this country are America's greatest ambassadors to the rest of the world. Since American music is listened to around the globe, royalties for works originally emanating from the U.S. are being earned almost everywhere on Earth that those songs are played.

Not wanting to miss out on opportunities to earn income from a song's use, publishers have devised methods by which they can be compensated for their works generating royalties on foreign soil, just as foreign copyright owners receive royalties when their songs are recorded and performed in the United States.

Our government helped pave the way for enhancing this process when it agreed to make the United States a party to the Universal Copyright Convention in 1955 and the Berne Convention in 1989. Under the terms of these multinational conventions—as well as the World Intellectual Property Organization treaties of 1996—many countries give copyrights created in the United States the same protection as their own domestic copyrights.

There are some countries that aren't a party to the conventions mentioned above. Some of these nonmember nations have direct treaties with the United States; the Copyright Office officially lists some other countries' copyright relationships with the United States as "unclear"; and a few countries have no copyright agreements with the United States at all.

Going through detailed explanations of which countries recognize U.S. copyrights under which specific treaties would be a lengthy and boring exercise. Argentina, Australia, Belgium, Brazil, France, Germany, Holland, Italy, Japan, Mexico, Spain, the United Kingdom, and many other countries recognize U.S. copyrights. Countries such as Iran, Iraq, and Afghanistan don't. At this point in history, it's a safe assumption that there aren't too many American pop songs being played in Iran, Iraq, or Afghanistan, so U.S. publishers probably aren't missing out on large sums of royalties there.

The main method of acquiring royalties from countries that do recognize U.S. copyrights is through a process called *subpublishing*. For example, if my publishing company owns a copyright that becomes a hit in England, I need to have an agreement with a British publishing company so it can collect royalties earned on the song in the United Kingdom. Based on the conditions of my company's agreement with the British firm, that company (known as the subpublisher) will pay my publishing company a percentage of all of the monies it collects for the song originally published by my company in the United States.

The concept of subpublishing is actually rather simple. In execution, however, it tends to become confusing because there are a variety of different routes a U.S. publishing company can take to acquire proper foreign representation. On top of that, subpublishing agreements can vary widely. Add to this the difficulty of dealing with a language barrier, foreign currencies, and publishing partners who are thousands of miles away, and you can begin to see how the simple concept of subpublishing can become extremely complicated.

TWO MAIN AVENUES OF FOREIGN REPRESENTATION

When a song is a hit in the United States, there is frequently foreign activity on the work as well. If a hit song belongs to a new publishing company in the United States, the new publisher will need to determine how he wishes to have his company represented in other countries. The U.S. publisher has two primary choices for foreign representation: (1) country-by-country (or, more accurately, territory-by-territory) subpublishing agreements, or (2) a single, worldwide subpublishing agreement with a multinational subpublisher—a company that already has subpublishing agreements in place or owns its own subpublishing companies around the world.

There are advantages and disadvantages to each of these choices. First, let's consider the advantages of territory-by-territory subpublishing agreements. If a song originating in the United States becomes a hit in England, the U.S. publisher can negotiate an agreement with a British subpublisher whereby the British company agrees to pay an advance to the American publisher. If the song becomes a hit in Germany a few weeks later, the U.S. publisher can then enter into a subpublishing agreement with a German publisher, acquiring another advance from the German publisher for the right to represent the song in his territory. As the song becomes a hit around the world, the U.S. publisher can continue to negotiate deals with publishers in each new country the song reaches, collecting advances from the individual subpublishers until the song has achieved worldwide representation.

Since there will probably be several companies in each country vying for subpublishing rights to the song, the U.S. publisher will usually have the upper hand in the negotiating procedures. In the end, he will come away with advances from each country and—if he has a good entertainment lawyer—the best possible deal from each of the subpublishers.

On the other hand, the U.S. publisher will now have well over a dozen subpublishing agreements to keep track of, complicated by the fact that each agreement will have different terms, different advances, and different royalty percentages to be collected. Also, if there is a dispute about payments due from, say, Scandinavia, a lawsuit would probably prove to be impractical.

The U.S. publisher's other choice for representation would be a large, multinational publishing company that already has representation outside of the United States. If a song becomes a hit abroad, the song's U.S. publisher would need to sign only one agreement to cover the entire world. A single subpublishing agreement usually dictates the same terms for each of the countries involved. If a problem arose in a particular foreign country, the U.S. publisher could require the administrating multinational publisher to resolve the problem.

The major disadvantage of a single, worldwide administration agreement is that the U.S. publisher would receive only one advance for the entire world, and this advance would, in all likelihood, be substantially less than the total of all advances the song's U.S. publisher could have acquired on a territory-by-territory basis. Then there is the matter of how much attention the U.S. publisher's song will receive. After all, the administrating multinational publisher has a catalog of its own songs to worry about—songs that may be making far more money for it than it will earn from simply representing someone else's song in foreign countries for a small percentage.

Although the U.S. publisher might be receiving less of an advance from a multinational publisher, having several subpublishers is a very time-consuming exercise. Therefore, the U.S. publisher could end up with essentially the same amount of money in either situation once the song's initial success has run its course.

A THIRD AVENUE OF FOREIGN REPRESENTATION

The U.S. publisher has a third option for collecting foreign royalties, although it is not a route commonly chosen by many publishers. A U.S. publisher affiliated with the Harry Fox Agency may request that HFA collect foreign royalties via its agreements with foreign collection societies and agencies. The advantage of using HFA is that no percentage of the royalties must be given up to a subpublisher. However, there are several disadvantages, including the fact that there are no advances offered, no exploitation (promotion) of the publisher's songs, and no attempts to acquire foreign language recordings. Most U.S. publishers are willing to allow subpublishers a larger percentage of royalty income than the Harry Fox Agency receives in exchange for an advance and the other available amenities.

THE TERRITORY-BY-TERRITORY APPROACH

If a U.S. publisher decides to take the territory-by-territory approach to subpublishing, he will be entering into a series of agreements with various subpublishers. For each agreement, there will be several points of negotiation to consider.

If a song is released in England, the U.S. publisher will probably be contacted by several publishers wishing to represent the song in their territory (United Kingdom, Ireland, etc.). The decision of which one of these companies will act as subpublisher for the song is usually based on which company has the best reputation or which offers the best deal. Ideally, both qualities will belong to the same company.

Some issues that should be considered by the U.S. publisher are: the amount of the advance; the term (or duration) of the subpublishing agreement; and the percentage of royalties to be retained by the subpublisher in exchange for services rendered.

The amount offered as an advance will depend on the country in question. Obviously a U.K. subpublisher would offer more than a subpublisher in another, much less active country. It will be up to the U.S. publisher to determine if any of the U.K. firms are offering a reasonable advance based on recent offers to other American publishers in similar circumstances. If the U.S. publisher doesn't have knowledge of other recent deals, he will either have to assume that the highest offer is a reasonable advance or rely on the expertise of an entertainment lawyer who is familiar with the current advances being negotiated in the United Kingdom.

However, the highest advance doesn't necessarily mean it is the best deal. The U.S. publisher must also negotiate the type of royalties the subpublisher will collect and the percentages of those royalties the subpublisher will retain.

Using the territory-by-territory approach doesn't necessarily mean making subpublishing agreements only with independent companies in foreign countries. All of the multinational companies (EMI, BMG, etc.) own individual companies in each of the major foreign territories. A U.S. publishing company can choose to use independent subpublishers in, say, England and Australia, while going with a major multinational company in other areas such as EMI in South America, BMG in France, and Warner/Chappell in some of the other international markets.

According to Gary Ford, former Manager of Foreign Administration for Warner/Chappell Music, publishers considering a territory-by-territory approach to subpublishing need to carefully evaluate potential subpublishers:

> *In an ideal situation, a publisher should actually visit the office of the intended subpublisher, meet the administrative and creative staff, and get an overall feeling for how they communi-*

cate and transact business. He should check their computer systems, royalty statement formats, etc.

Also, if the publisher wants his catalog exploited in the local market, it is often best to go with independent subpublishers, as they focus primarily on exploitation of their clients' catalogs and have excellent track records for obtaining local covers. (In music publishing lingo, exploitation is synonymous with plugging or promoting a song.)

However, the independents also have a reputation for not being the best administrators; hence the reasoning for either visiting the particular office or relying on an attorney you can trust to choose the best independent to suit your needs.

Gary feels that these points "are equally as important as an advance when deciding to do deals on a country-by-country basis. Each publisher has different needs, so an advance or rate split should not be the sole determining factor in choosing a subpublisher."

Connie Ambrosch-Ashton, who oversees the foreign interests of Leiber & Stoller Music Publishing and is Vice President of PEN Music Group, adds:

In my experience, a publisher can expect to receive a higher level of service by entering into territory-by-territory agreements rather than by entering into a single multinational deal, regardless of whether the subpublishers are independents, multinationals, or a combination. When you sign with someone for a particular territory, you can gage the level of enthusiasm for your music. It's this that translates into effort on the part of your subpublisher.

An enthusiastic subpublisher will do more than just the basics of registering your copyrights and collecting your income. They'll work to secure local covers and to get film and television placements, and they can often assist in arranging for local release of your U.S. product. Multinational deals always seem to be primarily about the advance money. I'm not sure how much anyone can realistically expect to get from a subpublisher on the other side of the world who's looking after a catalog only because someone in their U.S. office picked up the rights as part of a bigger deal. Many multinational deals originating out of the U.S. are the result of relationships between the U.S. office and an attorney—not passion for the music.

Choosing subpublishers is complex. Beyond the actual terms of the agreement there are other things to consider, such as what your goals are. What do you hope to accomplish by entering into the agreement? Are you just looking for someone to collect your royalties, or do you want someone who will play an active role in developing your career overseas? You should make it clear to the subpublishers you speak with what your expectations are in order to avoid disappointment later on.

If you're someone who doesn't want to spend time answering faxes and e-mails from around the world, a multinational deal may be best for you. This arrangement will generally put you in touch with a point person in your own country with whom you can communicate. That person's job is to ensure that the information given to them by you (such as new songs, new releases, cue sheets) gets to the right people in each of the applicable offices.

If you want to have more communication and feedback, you would probably be happier taking a hands-on approach by making a territory-by-territory deal in which you are in direct contact with each office. An advance can be a compelling reason to enter into a multinational deal, or to seek out independent publishers and multinationals able to give advances for individual territories. Again, don't be afraid to tell your prospective subpublishers what you're looking for.

Subpublishers generally issue licenses and collect royalties for mechanical reproductions, synch uses, printed editions, and (sometimes) the publisher's share of performance royalties. The portion of royalties the subpublisher retains is usually around 10 to 20 percent. If the subpublisher causes a recording to be made in his territory (this is generally referred to as a *local cover*), he frequently is allowed to keep a larger percentage of the royalties earned on that particular release than he keeps for recordings he wasn't responsible for (such as those that were already in existence at the time the subpublishing agreement was entered into).

THE SUBPUBLISHING SCENARIO

Snoop Beagle Music Publishing Company owns the song "I Love My Dog." Mr. Beagle makes a subpublishing deal for his catalog with a French company in which the French subpublisher will retain 10 percent of the royalties it collects on the original American recording of "I Love My Dog" in France. The French publisher is also given the right to adapt or translate the song into French so that he can have a better opportunity to exploit the song in his country. Although the foreign language version will still be copyrighted in the name of the U.S. publisher, the French publisher will be able to retain 20 percent of the royalties on either the English or French version of the song if he causes a recording of it to be made in his territory.

Let's say "I Love My Dog," as recorded by the American band Herman's Mutts, is an international hit. If the Mutts recording is released in France, that wouldn't qualify the French publisher to retain 20 percent of the royalties earned in France.

However, if the French publisher gets another act to record "I Love My Dog" (the English-language version) in France, he would retain 20 percent of the mechanicals received on that local cover. The same holds true if the French publisher gets a French act (let's call the band Bichon Frise) to record "J'aime Mon Bow Wow"—the French-language version of the song.

Assuming Snoop Beagle Music Publishing Company has a contract with the writer of "I Love My Dog" that calls for the songwriter to receive 50 percent of the mechanical income received by the publisher from foreign sources, the royalty payments would go like this:

The subpublisher in France receives the equivalent of $1,000 in mechanical royalties for Herman's Mutts' recording of "I Love My Dog." According to the subpublishing agreement, he retains $100 (10 percent) and pays the remaining $900 to Snoop Beagle's company. Snoop Beagle then pays $450 (50 percent of the mechanical income from the foreign sources) to the writer of "I Love My Dog."

When Bichon Frise's recording of "J'aime Mon Bow Wow" becomes a hit in France, the French publisher receives another $1,000 in mechanical royalties—this time for Bichon Frise's cover of the song. The subpublisher now retains $200 (20 percent) and pays $800 to Snoop Beagle Music Publishing. Mr. Beagle then pays $400 to the composer of "I Love My Dog" (once again, 50 percent of the income received by the American publisher from the foreign source).

What about the French writer who turned "I Love My Dog" into "J'aime Mon Bow Wow"? He receives mechanical royalties out of the 20 percent retained by the French publisher according to whatever deal the two of them have negotiated. He will also receive a portion of the song's performance royalty income reported in France, but only on the French-language version of the song.

The Subpublishing Agreement Term

Another area of consideration is the term of the subpublishing agreement. Years ago, subpublishers often acquired a song for the life of the copyright (which, in many countries, was life-plus-fifty). In some cases, subpublishers would retain the rights to a song for the first term of the U.S. copyright. As you can see, if a U.S. publisher became unhappy with a particular subpublisher, the results could be pretty devastating—the publisher would have already committed the song to that subpublisher for either life-plus-fifty or for a period of at least twenty-eight years. Since the life of a copyright is now life-plus-seventy in many foreign countries, the U.S. publisher who entered into a "life of copyright" deal a few decades ago lost the song outside the U.S. for twenty more years than he originally thought he would.

In more recent times, subpublishing deals have taken on more reasonable durations. Today, the common subpublishing term is usually around three years. The philosophy behind the three-year term is that the subpublisher will have plenty of time to show that he can exploit the song in his market, but not so much time that the remaining points of the deal have a chance to become antiquated.

There was a time when the subpublisher retained 50 percent of all income collected, as opposed to the 10 to 20 percent usually retained today. Many American publishers now find themselves locked into those old fifty-fifty deals for the life of their copyrights because those types of arrangements were very common until the early 1970s. Luckily for U.S. publishers and songwriters, such deals don't happen anymore with legitimate subpublishers.

Another major point of negotiation is the rights being granted to the subpublisher. The subpublisher usually has the right to collect mechanical, synch, and print royalties (and sometimes performance royalties). However, in a normal, pro-U.S. publisher deal, the subpublisher does not acquire the copyright itself in the subpublisher's territory. The publisher is merely allowing the subpublisher to act on the publisher's behalf.

In non-English-speaking countries, as pointed out in earlier in this chapter, the American publisher will usually allow the subpublisher the right to have translations or adaptations of the English lyrics created (to be approved by the publisher and, sometimes, the songwriter) so that the subpublisher will be in a better position to promote the song. The U.S. publisher should own the copyright to these new versions of the works; otherwise, if he decides to change subpublishers, the original subpublisher may claim to own rights to the adapted versions of the songs in the catalog. Two versions of the same song in the same country would be difficult to exploit, and payment of royalties would be confusing at best.

The number of songs the subpublisher acquires depends on the individual deal. A subpublisher may be granted the rights to a single song, to all of the songs the U.S. publisher acquires

Performance Royalty Income From Foreign Sources

The U.S. publisher's share of foreign performance royalties is usually a point of discussion in subpublishing deals because there are two possible ways for the publisher to receive foreign performance income.

One way that payment is handled is for the subpublisher to collect the U.S. publisher's foreign performance royalties directly from the foreign performing rights society with which the subpublisher is affiliated. The subpublisher then pays the publishing company its share of foreign performance income when he accounts to the publisher for all types of royalties due.

The other possible method of payment is for the foreign performing rights society to pay the publisher's (and songwriter's) share of foreign performance royalties directly to the proper performing rights society in America. That society then pays the publisher and songwriter.

Which of these two methods is best for the publisher is open to debate. In the first case mentioned above, the subpublisher is going to get to keep a portion of the U.S. publisher's performance royalty income, which—on the surface—would appear to be a disadvantage to the publisher.

On the other hand, the publisher is more likely to receive his foreign performance royalties sooner with this method, since the foreign performing rights society is paying the publisher's performance royalties directly to the subpublisher, which in turn pays the publisher the next time royalty accountings are due.

In the second scenario, the American publisher doesn't have to lose the percentage of performance royalty income that would have been taken out by the subpublisher. The disadvantage, though, is that foreign performing rights societies generally take a long time to pay U.S. performing rights societies. It also takes time for the U.S. societies to enter all of the foreign information into their computer systems. The publisher sometimes receives the foreign performance royalties from his affiliated U.S. performing rights society over a year after they were collected by the foreign performing rights society.

In the end, if this is a negotiable deal point, the publisher will have to determine which method he prefers. Of course, the subpublisher is going to want to collect the foreign performance royalties himself, since this means more money will go into his pocket.

Whatever the manner in which the publisher is paid foreign performance royalties, the U.S. songwriter almost always receives foreign performance royalties from his domestic performing rights society. In recent years, some songwriters have chosen to become members of a few of the larger foreign performing rights organizations (PRS in the U.K., SACEM in France, etc.) so they can be paid directly by the various societies with which they are affiliated. However, there's a great deal of paperwork involved, as well as foreign tax issues, so—for now—this practice remains quite rare.

during the term of the subpublishing agreement, or to any and all of the songs in the publisher's catalog that haven't already been assigned to another subpublisher in that particular territory.

If a subpublisher is acquiring the rights to an American publisher's catalog that contains several hits, the American publisher should be able to strike a much better deal than another American publisher who is offering only one song for subpublication.

Of course, a U.S. publisher with several hits could make deals with various subpublishers in the same territory on a song-by-song basis, acquiring advances from each subpublisher that might total more than the single advance offered by one subpublisher for all of the songs. But then the U.S. publisher might find himself buried under tons of paperwork, trying to keep track of who subpublishes what song in which territory—which leads us to the other main subpublishing option available to the U.S. publisher.

Single Worldwide Subpublishing

A single worldwide subpublishing agreement is usually made with a multinational subpublisher—a major publishing company that either already has subpublishing deals in place throughout the world or owns its own subpublishing companies around the globe.

Although the publisher would receive only one overall advance—as opposed to advances from each country—a major benefit of the single worldwide subpublishing agreement is that it is much simpler and easier to maintain. Also, by going with this approach, the publisher has only one deal to negotiate. And he will usually receive one foreign royalty statement twice a year that covers the entire world, rather than many different statements from various territories at different times during a twelve-month period.

As Gary Ford explains, "There are many other advantages of going with a multinational subpublisher: They usually have a better working relationship with their local performing rights societies due to their size; their computer systems are normally more up-to-date; and their professional staff is better equipped to deal with areas not usually addressed by the independent subpublisher."

The various negotiating points of the worldwide subpublishing agreement are very similar to those in a single-territory subpublishing agreement. However, the U.S. publisher has to take care to protect himself against a practice known as *double dipping*, which results in the U.S. publisher receiving a much smaller percentage of royalties than he is expecting. In the past, many U.S. publishers have been duped by subpublishers with whom they have entered into worldwide agreements. Although this is not a practice among the well-known and well-respected multinational subpublishers, it apparently still takes place among a few companies. Here's how it works.

U.S. publisher A enters into a worldwide subpublishing agreement with publisher B, who owns publishing companies around the world. B agrees to pay A 80 percent of the royalties B receives from its subpublishers. (Remember, these are companies that B owns.) Meanwhile, B has agreements with all of its subpublishers (essentially, agreements with itself) stating that the subpublishers will retain 50 percent of all sums received in their territories. So, if English subpublisher C receives $200 in royalties for a song in A's catalog, C retains $100 and sends $100 (50 percent) to B in the United States. B then pays $80 to A. Meanwhile, A was expecting to receive $160 (80 percent of $200).

There are several variations on this scheme, but the end result is always the same: publisher A receives substantially less in subpublishing royalties than his agreement would seem to indicate. To avoid this problem, a good entertainment lawyer makes certain that the worldwide subpublishing agreement calls for royalties to be computed *at the source*. In other words, if the subpublishing agreement is a 20 percent collection deal, each subpublisher must report the amount earned in his territory, of which 80 percent is to be received by publisher A when royalties are paid.

A Final Word on Subpublishing

Subpublishing is more important today than it has ever been. The royalties earned abroad on an international hit originating in the United States can sometimes be equal to or more than the amount earned in this country.

In the past, American publishers put the most emphasis on the amount of the advance they could get from a subpublisher, without worrying about how much that song might eventually earn in a foreign territory. In fact, after the initial large advance, the publishers often left the subpublisher to his own devices.

Today, subpublishers have become very competitive. Because the term of most subpublishing agreements is short, subpublishers work harder to exploit U.S. publishers' songs so their agreements will be renewed on a continuing basis.

Finally, it is interesting to note that the Internet might prove to be an extremely important factor in the future of subpublishing. By virtue of the fact that the Web is, indeed, worldwide, U.S. publishers are now capable of promoting their catalogs over the Internet. With that in mind, it's conceivable that the day could come when U.S. publishers would also be able to administer and collect royalties from foreign sources without the help of today's conventional subpublisher. What will happen to the entire concept of subpublishing in the years ahead depends almost entirely upon where expanding technology will lead us.

PART FOUR

The Songwriter's Contract and Publishing Options

TEN

The Single-Song Contract

Every published songwriter I have ever known has regretted at least one publishing agreement she has signed. In a lot of cases, that regret was justified. In others, if the writer hadn't signed the contract as written (or with a minimum of changes), the song probably wouldn't have been recorded at all, and the songwriter's career might not have gotten off the ground.

The fact is, if you are an unknown, never-had-a-song-recorded songwriter, it is highly unlikely that the very first agreement you sign will be as favorable as the agreement a songwriter with several hits is going to sign. Keep in mind that you shouldn't necessarily expect to start your career at the top. A young college graduate seeking employment is not going to walk into the personnel office at Microsoft and apply for the president's job. It's much more likely that she'll start near the bottom and slowly work her way upward.

Luckily, in the music business, rising to the top might not take nearly as long as in other businesses. But getting there is still probably going to require some compromises on your part. Your advantage will be that you are well-informed, because you are about to learn what many of your options are. And even the subtlest difference in the type of agreement you sign can mean a significant difference in royalties earned on a hit song.

Throughout this chapter, we'll discuss the various types of publishing agreements generally available to a songwriter. Let's start with the most common type of agreement between a songwriter and a publisher, the single-song contract.

An Overview

The single-song contract is an agreement between a music publisher and a songwriter in which the songwriter grants certain rights to a publisher for one or more songs. In acquiring these rights, the music publisher usually provides an advance against future royalties and agrees to promote uses of the song that will earn income for both parties. (The phrase *single-song contract* is another music publishing misnomer. One single-song contract can include several songs, all of which are individually subject to the clauses in the agreement.)

This type of agreement goes all the way back to the beginning of music publishing. In the days before radio, records, movies with sound, and television, the single-song contract between writer and publisher pertained only to sheet music and the amount of money the publisher would pay the songwriter for each copy of sheet music sold.

A few years ago I was given a copy of a single-song contract from the late nineteenth century. The entire contract looked something like the document on page 92.

Even in the late 1800s, single-song contracts could be a little confusing. The particular contract I have is for four cents on each copy sold, and the contract indicates that four cents is 10 percent. This meant that the retail price of the sheet music was forty cents. The agreement goes on to say "settlements" (royalty payments) will be made on January 1 and July 1. (Remarkably, there are still single-song contracts being written today that call for the writer to receive just a few cents per copy on sheet music sales, even though the retail price on sheet music is now ten times what it was in the late 1800s.)

Single-song contracts have undergone a lot of changes in the past century. Many single-song contracts today consist of several paragraphs that attempt to cover all possible types of royalties from all kinds of sources, including sources not yet in existence. Some songwriters complain about the length and complexity of today's single-song contract. However, all of the provisions that now exist in these contracts evolved out of precedent-setting events—including technological advances—over a period of decades. For example, today's smart songwriters insist that an audit clause be included in the single-song contract. In the 1800s a publisher could tell a songwriter that one thousand pieces of sheet music were sold when the true amount was actually ten thousand. If the songwriter's contract didn't guarantee the right to audit the publisher's books, the songwriter stood a good chance of losing out on a lot of money.

So, instead of complaining about the length and technical wording of a contract, the songwriter should learn what the single-song contract is all about. A properly constructed agreement can protect both the writer and the publisher in any given situation.

There is no such thing as a standard song contract, despite the fact that many publishers have contracts with the word *standard* in the heading. Any time a publisher offers a "standard contract" without allowing the songwriter the right to negotiate certain points of the agreement, it's time for the songwriter to seriously question the intentions of the publisher. (See the appendix for a copy of the Songwriters Guild of America's Popular Songwriters Contract. It's an excellent example of an agreement that is fairer to the songwriter than the average publisher's standard contract.)

Although the wording differs from one single-song contract to another, most of the contracts have standard language regarding the advance, royalty payments, copyright ownership, the writer's warrant that the song is an original work, and so on. Here are some characteristics common to all legitimate single-song contracts.

Advances

The reason a publisher wants a songwriter to sign a single-song contract is that the publisher believes that she can earn income on the song through successful exploitation. In exchange for obtaining certain rights to that song, the publisher should be willing to offer the songwriter an advance. An *advance* is a sum of money paid to the songwriter in anticipation of the future royalties the song will earn—effectively, it is payment of royalties in advance. The publisher will collect and keep all the royalties until the advance has been paid back (or *recouped*), then will begin sharing the royalties with the songwriter.

If the publisher asks that the songwriter pay *her*, then the songwriter isn't dealing with a true

Royalty Contract

New York, _____ 18 _____

We hereby agree to pay

_____
[author of song]

the sum of _____ cents (_____ per cent)

on each copy sold of a _____
[vocal or instrumental]

composition entitled:

_____

Settlements to made the first day of every

_____

_____
Signed

_____
Publisher

publisher. As we discussed before, anyone who demands money from a songwriter to acquire publishing rights to a song is known in the industry as a *song shark*. Any agreement that demands payment rather than offering an advance is not a legitimate single-song contract.

This is not to say that every single-song contract offers an advance to the songwriter. A new publishing company may be too small to offer an advance. The publisher's argument might be that, since the company is small and "hungry," the publisher will work much harder to get the song cut than would a giant company that deals with thousands of songs and songwriters—and the results from increased effort will make up for the lack of an advance. Such an argument might be viable. Under such circumstances, though, the new publisher should be willing to offer a better overall deal than a more established publisher who is willing to write an advance check.

The actual amount of a single-song contract advance varies widely among publishers, so it's impossible for me to give you a specific dollar figure. Sometimes it's $1,000; other times it's less; other times it's more. It all depends on the publisher in question and the publisher's belief in the song's hit potential. By offering an advance, the publisher is showing that she is willing to gamble real money on her ability to get your song recorded.

Whatever the amount of the advance, it is *recoupable* according to most single-song contracts. In fact, the language describing the advance in the contract is usually along the lines of "a nonreturnable, recoupable advance in the amount of $_____." Although *nonreturnable* and *recoupable* seem contradictory, what this phrase actually means is: (1) The songwriter will receive an advance of *x* dollars. (2) The advance is nonreturnable: If the song doesn't earn any royalties for the duration of the agreement, the songwriter doesn't pay the amount of the advance back to the publisher when the agreement expires. (3) The advance *is* recoupable: If the song gets recorded and earns back the amount of the advance or more, the publisher gets to recoup the advance, after which all other monies earned on the song are split between the publisher and the songwriter according to their agreement.

The only songwriter's royalty that the publisher can't recoup is performance royalty income, which is paid directly to the songwriter by his performing rights society. Of course, the publishing company is receiving its share of performance royalties directly as well. However, the single-song contract usually states that the advance is to be recouped from the songwriter's share of income. Therefore, the publisher isn't likely to count his own performance royalty income as money earned back against the songwriter's advance.

Transfer of Rights

In chapter three we discussed the six exclusive rights of the copyright owner. Generally, most of these exclusive rights are transferred by the songwriter to the music publisher in a single-song contract. In exchange, the songwriter gets an advance, a guarantee that the publisher will make a best effort to exploit the song, and approximately 50 percent of all royalties actually earned by the song.

One of the commonly used phrases referring to this transfer in a single-song contract is "The writer hereby sells, assigns, transfers, and delivers" (the copyright to the publisher). Theoretically, the writer could sell, assign, transfer, and deliver each of her six exclusive rights to one of six separate parties. However, since mass confusion would reign in such a situation, a writer usually transfers all of her rights in a song to one particular publisher.

The exception to this rule arises when a songwriter co-publishes a song with another publisher or assigns administration rights to an administrator. We will discuss these alternatives in chapter twelve.

The Songwriter's Royalties

In general, single-song contracts are offered only to songwriters without a track record. Songwriters who are already successful to some degree are usually offered other types of agreements with higher royalty rates.

In the previous chapters, we discussed the various types of royalties received by publishers, all of which are covered in the single-song contract (with the possible exception of grand rights. The royalties that are shared between the publisher and the songwriter—mechanical royalties, synchronization royalties, new media royalties, and royalties received by the publisher from foreign sources—are usually split approximately fifty-fifty. In no case should a songwriter agree to accept less than 50 percent of the income received by the publisher from these sources. (See the royalty splits chart on page 96.) (As we discussed in chapter nine, the songwriter's share of foreign performance royalties is paid to the songwriter's U.S. performing rights society by the foreign society. The American society then pays the writer. In other words, the royalties received by the publisher from foreign sources don't include the songwriter's foreign performance income, so the publisher keeps all of the royalties it receives for foreign performance.)

There is one area, however, in which the publisher will usually end up with more than 50 percent of the income received. This royalty source is printed editions, in which case the songwriter is paid at one of a variety of rates depending on the type of edition in question and on whether the publisher also makes the printed editions or licenses those rights to a print publisher. (Sheet music royalties, for example, are usually stipulated as x cents for each copy sold or x percent of the wholesale selling price.) If the single-song contract calls for the writer to receive twenty cents per copy sold, and the publisher receives fifty cents per copy sold from the print publisher, then the songwriter is going to be paid less than 50 percent on sheet music royalties.

The same is true for other printed editions as well. The single-song contract may offer the songwriter 10 percent of the wholesale selling price of other printed editions of the composition (such as band, orchestra, and choral arrangements) when, in fact, the publisher is getting 25 percent or more of the wholesale price.

Royalties for folios can become even more confusing, since the amount paid to the writer depends on several factors. If the publisher prints his own folios, the royalty due the writer will be a percentage (usually 10 to 12.5 percent) of the wholesale selling price. If the publisher allows someone else to print a folio that includes the song referred to in the single-song contract, the songwriter's royalties will be a percentage (usually 50 percent) of what the publisher receives.

The Songwriters Guild of America

The Songwriters Protective Association (SPA) was formed in 1931 by three respected songwriters: Billy Rose ("It's Only a Paper Moon," "Me and My Shadow"), George W. Meyer ("For Me and My Gal"), and Edgar Leslie ("Moon Over Miami"). According to the Songwriters Guild of America Web site, these men created SPA for the purpose of taking actions that would "advance, promote, and benefit" the songwriting profession.

The following year, a Standard Uniform Popular Songwriters Contract was developed by SPA for members of the organization. This contract was created by songwriters as a fairer document than the types of contracts publishers were offering to most writers at that time.

The SPA is now known as the Songwriters Guild of America (SGA), and it is the largest and oldest songwriters' association in the country. SGA provides a variety of services to its members, including regional and online songwriting workshops, regional and online song critique sessions, contract reviews, royalty collections (excluding performance royalties), audits of publishers, catalog administration—even group medical and life insurance. The Guild also continues to issue its own songwriter's contract.

SGA is governed by a council made up of professional songwriters. Although there are many expenses involved in the operation of the organization, Guild council members are all volunteers. The expenses incurred are covered by annual membership dues and a commission charged on royalties collected from publishers on behalf of SGA members.

The Guild currently offers three types of membership: gold (for unpublished writers who are just starting out); platinum (for unpublished writers who are further along in their writing careers); and diamond (for published songwriters). More information on the Songwriters Guild of America is available at songwritersguild.com, or by writing the association at 1500 Harbor Blvd., Weehawken, NJ, 07086-6732. The phone number is (201) 867-7603; their fax number is (201) 867-7535. A copy of the Guild contract, along with an overview of the agreement's major clauses, appears in the appendix.

In either case, the amount paid to the writer will be *pro rata* (determined by the number of songs in the folio).

For example, if the publisher prints a folio that contains twenty songs, one of which belongs to a songwriter who is contracted to receive 12.5 percent of the wholesale selling price, that songwriter will receive 12.5 percent of one-twentieth of the wholesale price. If the wholesale price is ten dollars, the songwriter would receive 6.25 cents for each copy sold (ten dollars divided by twenty, times 12.5 percent).

On the other hand, let's say a music publisher has a print deal with a print publisher. The print publisher puts out a folio containing twelve songs, two of which belong to the music publisher. One of the two songs is written by a songwriter who receives 50 percent of the publisher's receipts on a pro rata basis. In this case, the songwriter will receive 50 percent of half of the royalties earned by the music publisher from the folio (half of the music publisher's royalties times 50 percent).

In today's music publishing world, print income usually takes a back seat to most other royalty streams, so making less than 50 percent of what the publisher receives from sheet music and folios isn't really all that traumatic. On the other hand, it never hurts to try to use a bit of reverse psychology. If I were a songwriter about to sign a single-song contract with a publisher who uses an outside print publisher, I would argue that we should split the print income equally—especially in light of the fact that it's not going to be a major source of income for either party in the first place.

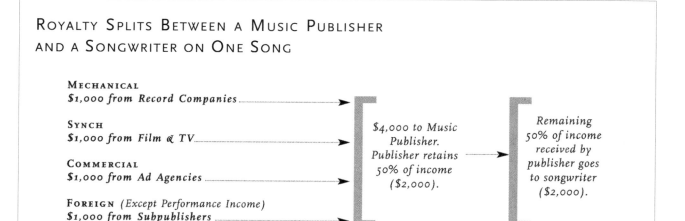

ROYALTY SPLITS BETWEEN A MUSIC PUBLISHER
AND A SONGWRITER ON ONE SONG

MECHANICAL
$1,000 from Record Companies

SYNCH
$1,000 from Film & TV

COMMERCIAL
$1,000 from Ad Agencies

FOREIGN *(Except Performance Income)*
$1,000 from Subpublishers

$4,000 to Music Publisher. Publisher retains 50% of income ($2,000).

Remaining 50% of income received by publisher goes to songwriter ($2,000).

This chart assumes that the songwriter has recouped any outstanding advances and that the publisher's single-song contract calls for the writer to receive 50 percent of the royalties—foreign and domestic—from the four income sources listed. (The foreign performance royalties [not shown] are paid to the publisher's and songwriter's U.S. performing rights society, which then pays both the writer and the publisher their shares of performance royalties directly.)

Territory Covered

The single-song contract almost always grants the publisher worldwide rights to the song in question. This gives the publisher the greatest possible chance of earning income on the song either by adding it to the songs that are already part of a subpublishing agreement or by assigning the song to various subpublishers throughout the world.

The Term of the Contract

When a songwriter signs a single-song contract, she is allowing one publisher to acquire the rights to one or more songs for a certain period of time. The *term* of a single-song contract is the specific amount of time that the contract will be in effect. This length of time will be determined by several factors. Before the 1976 Copyright Act went into effect, there were generally two possible terms a songwriter could agree to: the first term of U.S. copyright (twenty-eight years) or the life of copyright including the renewal term (fifty-six years). The 1976 law changed the life of the copyright to the life of the author plus fifty years, but stipulated a writer could terminate an agreement with a publisher at the end of thirty-five years (if the song had been published) or forty years from the date of the agreement, whichever was shorter. If the writer and/or his heirs wished, however, the song could remain with the original publisher for the rest of the copyright's life (which is now life-plus-seventy). In such a case, the publisher would usually have to pay an advance or bonus (a bonus is nonrecoupable) in order to retain the copyright.

Of course, in a single-song contract, the writer and publisher can agree to whatever amount of time they wish, up to the maximum allowed by copyright law. If Wanda the writer convinces Pete the publisher that Pete should have the song for only a decade, then the term of the single-song contract would be ten years. If the contract included a *reversion clause* (see below), then the term of the contract might be even shorter.

The Reversion Clause

As I have said before, the act of signing a contract with a music publisher doesn't mean a song is now published. A song is only published when it is recorded in some fashion and distributed for sale. In the single-song contract, the publisher is sometimes given a specific amount of time to acquire a recording of the song in question. For instance, the contract may state that the publisher has one year to get the song cut. At the end of one year from the date of the contract, if the publisher has not been successful in her efforts, all rights to the song revert to the writer. The portion of the single-song contract that spells out the songwriter's right to regain the copyright is called the *reversion clause*. Some reversion clauses stipulate that the writer has to return the advance and/or the publisher's demo costs.

The amount of the advance the publisher offers might depend on the length of time the publisher is allowed to get the song recorded. For instance, a publisher who has only six months before a reversion clause goes into effect is probably going to offer a lower advance (if any) than a publisher would who has a year or eighteen months to get the song used.

Some single-song contracts contain another reversion clause that states that the copyright reverts back to the songwriter if the publisher fails to pay royalties properly or on time. (See the Songwriters Guild contract in the appendix.)

Accounting and Audit Clauses

Earlier we covered the topic of royalties to be paid to the writer by the publisher. Elsewhere in the single song contract there is a paragraph that explains how often and at what time during the fiscal or calendar year the publisher will make these royalty payments. Generally, royalty payments will be made twice a year at six-month intervals, usually within forty-five days of the end of each six-month period. Assuming the publisher pays based on the calendar year, the writer should expect to be paid around the middle of August (forty-five days after June 30) and again around the middle of February (forty-five days after December 31).

For the songwriter's protection, the contract should also contain an audit clause that allows the writer (or her financial representative) to examine the publisher's books once a year to make certain that royalty payments are accurate. Many publishers honestly attempt to make proper payments. Those that don't make payments on time usually develop a reputation that prevents writers from wanting to sign agreements with them in the future. Sometimes, though, publishers (or their royalty departments) do make mistakes, so even the most honest of publishers can, on occasion, pay a writer less than she is actually due. For this reason, a publisher should be willing to include an audit clause in the single-song contract.

Warranty, Indemnity, and Disputes

These three topics are all a part of the common single-song contract. The warranty section applies to the writer, who is required to warrant (or guarantee) that she is transferring the rights to an original work of authorship to the publisher, and that she hasn't already transferred those rights to any other publisher or third party.

The indemnity clause relates directly to the warranty clause and states that the writer will be held financially responsible for any lawsuits that might arise in case it turns out that, in fact, the song was actually written by someone else, or that the writer had already assigned the song to another publisher.

The disputes clause, on the other hand, refers to possible clashes between the writer and the publisher. Usually such disputes are over royalties and transpire shortly after the songwriter has had the publisher's books audited. Normally, this kind of dispute is resolved by proper payment from the publisher.

But what if the publisher refuses to pay what is obviously owed? Or what if the publisher refuses to grant an audit at all, even though the contract clearly states that she must? The disputes clause is included in the single-song contract to clarify how such a disagreement will be resolved. Many times it will state that the writer and publisher must agree to the resolution of disputes through binding arbitration (rather than through a lawsuit). Binding arbitration is the act of settling a dispute by putting the problem before a qualified, disinterested third party who decides how the dispute will be resolved.

ELEVEN

The Exclusive or Staff Writer Contract

The phrases *exclusive contract* and *staff writer contract* are two terms for an agreement in which the writer is signed exclusively to a particular publishing company. For the sake of brevity, let's refer to this agreement throughout this chapter as a staff writer contract.

Staff writer contracts are usually offered when a publisher believes, based on a writer's past success, that the songwriter's talents warrant a deal granting the publisher the rights to all of the songs written by the writer during the term of the contract. Sometimes these contracts are offered even when a writer's track record consists of only one or two recorded songs. In fact, this is usually the best time (from the publisher's point of view) to get a songwriter to sign such a deal. A songwriter with no previous success and a handful of songs might be considered too much of a risk by most publishers. A writer with several hits under her belt would demand a large weekly advance and a contract heavily in her favor. However, a writer with only a cut or two to her name is the perfect type for a publisher to approach with an offer of a staff writer agreement.

A songwriter who has a staff writer contract with a publisher is like an artist contracted to a particular record label. As long as the artist is signed to that label, she can't go out and make a record for a rival company.

Advances

One of the major differences between the single-song contract and the staff writer contract is the amount of advance money involved and the manner in which the advance is paid. When a writer signs a single-song contract, she is paid a one-time recoupable advance. Advances are paid to the staff writer weekly, monthly, or (in rare instances) quarterly. A staff writer can sometimes draw, weekly, an amount equal to the one-time advance for a single-song contract. (But it should be noted that the weekly or monthly advances paid to a staff writer are recoupable, just as is the advance paid under the terms of a single-song contract.) The weekly advance paid to a staff writer is similar to the weekly draws paid to salespeople against commissions on future sales. The amount of the songwriter's weekly draw (or advance) will usually depend on the writer's (or the writer's lawyer's) negotiating power.

For example, a nonperforming songwriter with a minimal number of recorded songs generally has very little negotiating power. She is probably looking for a publisher willing to sign her to a staff writer agreement for a few hundred dollars a week so that she can make ends meet for the duration of the agreement while she writes full-time.

On the other hand, a writer who also has a recording contract will be offered a very high advance (potentially thousands of dollars per week). The publishing company knows that it has an excellent chance of recouping the advance and making a profit from an agreement with a writer/performer, since the writer is already planning to release an album filled entirely with her own songs.

Somewhere in between is the writer/performer who hasn't yet acquired a recording contract. As I have emphasized before, music publishing is no longer just a matter of finding a great song and trying to get it recorded. Granted, this is still an important part of the business, especially in Nashville. However, many music publishers (including those in Nashville) are on the lookout for the songwriter/performer who can be taken into the recording studio, where professional artist demos or even finished masters of the songwriter's original material can be made. The music publisher can then pitch the finished product to record labels in an attempt to turn the performing songwriter into a recording act. Thus, the publisher will often sign the writer/artist to a staff writer contract and attempt to get a recording contract for her so that the publisher will, once again, be in a position to reap a profit from the situation.

Publishers are almost always open to signing a writer who has a built-in guarantee that her songs will be recorded. This guarantee can come in the form of a signed or soon-to-be-signed recording contract, but a songwriter who is also a record producer with the power to get her own songs cut also carries a guarantee. Of course, as I said earlier, writers in these positions can demand a great deal of money and very favorable contract terms. They are also, in many cases, able to demand that *all* of the money they expect to receive during the term of the agreement be paid up front—an enviable situation to be in. (As we will see, writers in such powerful positions are much more likely to sign co-publishing or administration agreements than staff writer agreements.)

The Term of the Staff Writer Contract

There are generally three types of terms included in most staff writer agreements. The first of these three is the term of the contract itself. This is usually a one-year term with a specific series of one-year options. For example, a contract might call for a one-year deal with three one-year options, which means the publisher has the option to decide if she wishes to continue her relationship with the writer at the end of each year, for a maximum total contractual term of four years (the original one-year term plus the three options).

The second type of term is the length of time the publisher will retain ownership of the copyrights acquired during the term of the staff writer contract. In some cases this will be the same as in a single-song contract (approximately thirty-five years). In many modern-day staff writer agreements, publishers agree to shorter terms of five to twenty-five years. At the end of this term, the copyrights revert to the writer, who can sign a new deal with the publisher, assign the copyrights to another publisher, or assign the copyrights to his own publishing company.

The third term is the amount of time the publisher is allowed to try to get the songs in question recorded. Often this term will be the length of the staff writer agreement plus anywhere from one to five years. If there are songs that remain unrecorded after that time, many staff writer agreements allow the writer to "buy back" those copyrights for the amount of any unrecouped advances and the costs of the demos of the unrecorded songs.

Works Made for Hire

A work made for hire is "a work prepared by an employee within the scope of his or her employment. . . ." Some publishers consider songs written by a staff writer to be works made for hire, and therefore claim actual authorship of the work as the employer under the copyright law. These publishers' staff writer agreements usually state that all songs written during the term of the agreement will be considered works made for hire. Despite the fact that the copyright law says the employer will be considered the author of a work made for hire, the publisher will usually agree to credit the writer in the appropriate instances and allow the writer to receive the usual writer's share of all types of royalties. However, the copyright doesn't revert to the writer at the end of thirty-five years, since the copyright law clearly states that the employer is considered to be the author.

A songwriter who is offered a staff writer agreement should always have such language removed from the agreement. In fact, the writer should ask that the contract specifically state that any songs written during the term of the contract are *not* works made for hire.

Common Points in the Staff Writer Contract

Most of the other topics covered in the staff writer contract are similar to those in a single-song contract. A couple of other items common to the staff writer agreement are a statement of the specific number of songs required to be written, and inclusion of back catalog.

1. A staff writer deal will usually require that the writer turn over to the publisher a certain number of acceptable songs each year. The number of songs will vary, depending on the writer. However, the number of songs the writer agrees to turn out may affect the amount of advance money he is offered. Also, it's important to note that the concept of writing a certain number of songs isn't as straightforward as it might seem.

If a writer agrees to write twenty songs a year, he is agreeing that his share of the writing will total twenty complete songs. In other words, if that writer composes the melody to twenty songs, but someone else writes the lyrics, the contracted songwriter has only written twenty half-songs, or the equivalent of ten complete songs. He will have to write either twenty more melodies or ten more complete songs—or some combination of the two—so that the total amount of songs for the year will equal twenty complete songs.

You may have noticed that I specified that a songwriter is expected to turn in a certain amount of *acceptable* songs each year. What this means is that the songs must be deemed acceptable by the publisher. If a writer submits a song the publisher considers to be too weak to try to exploit, the writer will not be able to count it against the total number of songs required in his contract.

Of course, the writer who is also a recording artist is an exception to this rule. If he records the song and it's released on an album, it will obviously count in the total number of songs, no matter how bad the publisher might think it is.

2. The other topic common to staff writer agreements is the writer's back catalog. These are songs written prior to the signing of the staff writer contract. Often a writer will agree to include these titles in the contract if they are available and if they will count against the total number of songs required by the agreement. However, the writer obviously can't agree to include songs that are already signed to another publisher. Also, if the writer owns the publishing to a song that has already been successfully recorded, she is not likely to want to give up that song to another publisher.

The Recorded and Release Commitment

One of the most complicated and tempting conditions that many publishers include in their staff writer agreements is the awkwardly named recorded and release commitment. In fact, it's so complex that only a very good entertainment lawyer could possibly explain it. That being the case, here's attorney Jeffrey S. Sacharow's breakdown of precisely what this clause entails, and why you as a songwriter should be careful if a publisher asks you to sign an agreement containing recorded and release commitment language:

> *One way that publishers structure song delivery requirements under exclusive songwriter agreements is to provide for a recorded and release commitment. The recorded and release commitment is typically used by publishers when signing writer/producers or other songwriters who are not themselves recording artists.*
>
> *A recorded and release commitment obligates the writer to deliver to the publisher an agreed-upon number of musical compositions that will be recorded and commercially released nationally by a major record company.*
>
> *Since whether a record ends up being released is largely out of your (and your publisher's) control—and getting others to record your songs is usually a Herculean feat—most writers who have publishing deals containing release commitments do not guarantee the release of each of the songs they are required to deliver. A typical delivery requirement might be ten whole songs, of which four or five have to be recorded and commercially released.*
>
> *Publishers usually base the advances they are willing to pay you, in large part, on an estimate of what they think they will earn from your songs. Therefore, the more songs that you are willing to commit to being recorded and released, the higher your advance will likely be. Now, before you think,* Heck! I'll agree to twenty songs being released if I can get that big check, *know that most publishers will not require or accept a completely unrealistic release commitment.*
>
> *Now, this all seems easy, right? No sweat. You can easily crank out ten super smashes each year that anyone in her right mind would want to record. Not so fast. Even if you could write amazing songs each day, all day, getting them to count as part of your release commitment is difficult.*

Most publishers will only count your songs as one full released song under certain conditions.

1. *You must be the only writer of that song. If you are not the only writer of that song, most publishers will count the song as a partial song in proportion to your writer interest in that song. So, for example, if you have a five-song release commitment and you usually write with one other person, you will have to release ten of those co-written songs to fulfill your release commitment.*

2. *The song has to be contained on an album that is released throughout the United States by a so-called major record company. Again, this is not something in your control. Even if an artist signed to a major record deal agrees to record your song, there is no guarantee that the song will actually make the album, or that the album will ever be released.*

3. *The major record company must actually pay the publisher a full mechanical royalty rate. The latter requirement seems especially easy, but it is not. Various factors, including samples and controlled composition provisions, often reduce the mechanical royalty rate payable for the use of a particular song.*

Now, after reading all this, you are probably totally discouraged and thinking to yourself, Wait a minute. This is dang near impossible. Even if I can write all those amazing songs under the pressure of an agreement that requires me to write those songs, what's the point? There is no way I can control which songs get cut or even released. *You're right. You can't. But if you want the big (or bigger) advances, you are going to have to be willing to take the risk that you will be able to meet your release commitment. Be cautious, however, in determining what you realistically will be able to accomplish and what you agree to. If you cannot fulfill your commitment in the time period required under your publishing agreement, one of the remedies typically available to the publisher is to place you in what will seem like an indefinite limbo: They can extend the term of their agreement with you—with no further obligation to pay you any additional advances—until you have met your release commitment (which means, among other things, that you cannot write for any other publisher during this period of time).*

✤ TWELVE ✤

Co-Publishing and Administration Agreements

Co-publishing means exactly what the word implies: two or more publishers co-owning the rights to a particular song or group of songs. There are several different circumstances under which a song would be co-published.

For example, a successful songwriter may be offered a staff writer contract with a large advance in exchange for splitting the publisher's share with the established publisher who is offering the deal. In other words, the established publisher will own 50 percent of the publisher's share of income (as opposed to 100 percent) and will allow the writer to own the remaining 50 percent of the publisher's share (along with 100 percent of the writer's share). This type of agreement is now very commonplace. (As I have said before, why should a writer or writer/performer—especially a successful one—grant all of the publisher's share of income to an outside party?)

For her 50 percent interest in the publisher's share, the established publisher will usually handle all of the administrative and professional duties. When royalties are due, the writer/publisher will receive 75 percent of the income (all of the writer's share and half of the publisher's share), and the established publisher will retain 25 percent (her half of the publisher's share).

Another type of co-publishing situation occurs when two writers each own the publishing on their shares of a song they have written together. In this case, the two writers will either: (1) each administer her own publishing company; (2) determine which of the two publishing companies will act as administrator, or (3) hire an outside administrator.

If two writers who wrote songs together were signed to the same publisher, and one of the writers regained his share of the copyrights upon renewal (or for some contractual reason) while the other writer remained with the original publisher, there would now be two co-publishers co-owning the songs written together by the two writers.

Now let's say two writers are signed to staff writer agreements with two separate publishers. If these two writers (both of whom have co-publishing agreements with their publishers) decide to write a song together, there would then be four co-publishers of that song.

Keeping track of proper payments on such a song may seem a cumbersome task, but co-publishing is not at all uncommon. In the modern-day music business, many well-known songs have numerous publishers. There is one song among the catalogs I have managed that has nine co-publishers. If a song is co-written by all six members of a recording act, and each member has her own publishing company—and if that same song also samples two other songs that are each owned by multiple publishers—the total number of co-publishers of the resultant work can end up in double digits. As you can imagine, in those situations it's almost a miracle when everybody gets paid properly.

The percentage of a song a co-publisher owns depends entirely on the situation at hand. The most common type of co-publishing relationship is an equal split between the co-publishers. The manner in which royalties are disbursed among the co-publishers depends on the agreement (if any) entered into by the parties. For instance, in some cases the co-publishers draw up an agreement stating that one of the co-publishers will administer the copyright(s) in question. What this usually means is that one specific co-publisher will handle all of the licensing and collection of royalties and will then pay the amount due to the other co-publisher(s) on a quarterly or semiannual basis. The copyright law states that if there is no written agreement between the co-publishers, either or any of them can enter into a nonexclusive license as long as the other co-publishers are properly accounted to.

In other words, if a copyright is owned by co-publisher A and co-publisher B, co-publisher A can make a deal for the song to be used in a movie for $50,000 as long as co-publisher A then pays co-publisher B his share of the $50,000 (or has the film company pay co-publisher B his share directly).

If, on the other hand, an ad agency wants to use a song in a commercial exclusive to a particular product (e.g., dog food), and there is no written agreement between the co-publishers about how such situations are to be handled, all of the co-publishers would have to jointly agree to that exclusive use. Each co-publisher would then collect her share of the synch royalties directly from the party to whom the synch license was issued.

The important thing to note is that co-publishing is very much a part of the music business today. The manner in which all of the parties involved collect their shares of royalties must be determined either through a contract among all of the parties or by adherence to the copyright law.

Administration Agreements

An administration agreement is an arrangement between an administrator and a songwriter who owns 100 percent of the publishing on his songs. As I mentioned above, two songwriters who co-own the publishing rights to a song or songs may want to use an outside administrator as well.

Music publishing veteran Joan Schulman explains the function of an administrator.

> The independent administrator does all of the paperwork just like a publisher would: files copyright and renewal registrations; issues mechanical licenses; negotiates synch fees and issues synch licenses. The independent administrator also monitors the incoming payments. If a mechanical license is issued, for instance, the administrator makes sure that the money comes in when it's due. If it doesn't, it's the administrator's responsibility to follow up and make sure the money is paid.

MUSIC PUBLISHING MATH

Just as music publishing seems to have a language all its own, it appears to have also made up its own form of math. For the uninitiated, this math can be confusing since the total percentage of the publisher's and songwriter's shares on a particular song can be either 100 or 200 percent, depending on the type of royalty being discussed and who's discussing it.

Some forms of royalty income are referred to in fractions of 100 percent. This is because the publisher (assuming there are no co-publishers) receives 100 percent of the income from a particular source (such as mechanical royalties from a record company) and then divides the income between himself and the songwriter(s). The most common percentages for a song with one publisher and two writers would be referred to as indicated on the pie chart on the left.

In the case of performance royalties, however, the performing rights societies pay the publisher(s) and songwriter(s) their individual shares directly. A publisher who has no co-publisher(s) on a particular song receives a statement saying that he is receiving 100 percent of the publisher's share of the performance royalties for that song. The songwriter of that same song (assuming there is only one writer) receives a statement that also says 100 percent.

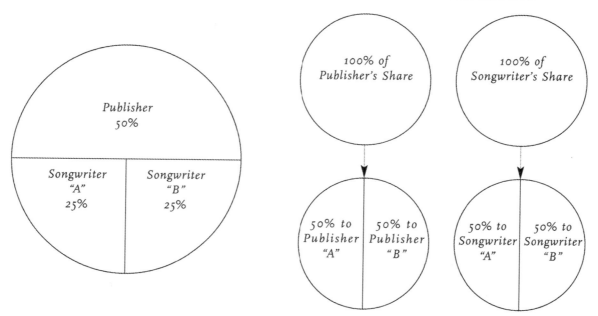

PERFORMANCE ROYALTIES DUE

When a publisher and a songwriter of a particular song receive performance royalty statements that indicate payments of less than 100 percent for each, this means that there is more than one publisher and more than one writer of that song. The pie charts on the right indicate that a performing rights society is paying royalties for a song with two co-publishers and two songwriters.

When you add up the publishers' and songwriters' shares of performance royalty income, the total comes to 200 percent. Although this is a simple concept, there is a natural tendency—among those of us who believe that it's hard to have more than 100 percent of something—to be confused when these strange percentages are discussed.

Perhaps the best way to look at this is from the songwriter's perspective. If you write half of a song and someone else writes the other half, you are going to take credit for 50 percent of the writing. So, if you add up your 50 percent, your partner's 50 percent, and your publisher's 100 percent of the publisher's share, you're back to 200 percent again. Welcome to the world of music publishing math.

In fact, an independent administrator does almost everything that a publisher would do except exploitation. After all, the title is administrator, *so it's not usually the independent administrator's job to shop songs.*

An administration deal can be made between a songwriter/publisher and an independent administrator or between a writer/publisher and another music publisher (who then handles the administrative duties for that writer/publisher as well as for the music publisher's own catalog).

In either case, the administrator usually doesn't participate in copyright ownership of the writer/publisher's songs. Instead, the administrator charges either a percentage (around 10 to 15 percent of the gross on royalties received) or an hourly fee for her services.

The Entertainment Lawyer

Throughout the centuries, lawyers have been dealt with rather harshly. Even the Bible has some unkind things to say about them: "Woe unto you also, ye lawyers. . . ." (Luke 11:46). Songwriter Kevin Bowe points out, "The music business is no different than any other; everyone hates lawyers, 'til they need one themselves!"

A common complaint in the music industry is that lawyers have practically taken over the business, either by running the business from behind the scenes or by actually being the heads of major music publishing and record companies. As one well-known songwriter/publisher once editorialized, there was a time when a member of the music industry would go to an entertainment attorney to get advice on how a company should be structured; at some point along the way, the lawyers stopped giving advice and just started running the companies themselves. Although some believe that the role of the entertainment lawyer in the music industry has become too great, the advice of a good entertainment lawyer is certainly advantageous to the songwriter who is trying to get the best possible protection and the best possible deal for his songs.

In an ideal world (to use a common lawyer's phrase) there would be no need for lawyers. But almost everyone involved in the music business would agree that things aren't exactly ideal out there. I cannot overemphasize the entertainment attorney's importance. No matter what stage a songwriter has reached in her career, an entertainment lawyer is the only type of lawyer to use. Real estate and divorce lawyers just won't do in the music business game. (The former will probably be needed if you become successful; the latter will probably be needed if you become *too* successful.) An experienced entertainment lawyer knows what standard practices are in the music industry and is able to help her songwriter clients through every legal aspect of a music publishing deal.

The best advice I can give on how to choose the right entertainment lawyer is to get recommendations from songwriters who are happy with their legal representation. If you don't know any successful songwriters, you should attend music industry workshops and seminars and ask the panelists for the names of respected lawyers in the business.

Rupert Holmes has strong feelings about the importance of entertainment lawyers:

I had a tendency in my first few years in the business to literally sign anything that was put in front of me. I was so afraid that I would offend someone by asking to read the contract or by taking it to a lawyer. I was so terrified that publishers might forever ignore me and that I would insult them so much. And, frankly, most of the time publishers have said, "Oh, why do you want to take it to a lawyer? Lawyers cause trouble."

There's usually a reason why publishers say that. If someone says, "Ah, don't bring a lawyer into this thing, because it'll just get so complicated and it'll cause problems," it means that in some way you're getting ripped off. If people object to you taking a contract to a lawyer, it isn't just because lawyers might make things complicated. It's because lawyers have a tendency to ask for things that might be appropriate.

But there's still always that pressure to sign, because you're afraid that the publisher will vanish. In this day and age, though, there really is no reason to rush that signature. If someone asks my advice, I just tell them to go slow in terms of signing, because when you sign contracts, those signatures don't go away—and they can loom large later on.

Holmes says there is another important reason to have a good entertainment lawyer: "Most of my best breaks in the business have come from attorneys and recording engineers. Choose your attorney very carefully. If you choose an attorney who's already negotiating with a major record label or publisher for five other artists . . . and he says, 'By the way, while I'm here, would you listen to this?' It can be a real good 'in' for you."

Lawyers aren't cheap. Perhaps that's one of the reasons they have to endure so much criticism. However, the amount of money they can keep you from losing will more likely than not justify the expense of their fees.

Call them a necessary evil or a godsend, one of the most important lessons you can learn from these pages is to get the best entertainment attorney you can afford. In fact, if you learn nothing else from this book than to hire a good entertainment lawyer before you sign that first contract (or that next contract), then I believe the cost of this book will have been worth it to you.

PART FIVE

*Music
Publishing
Companies*

☙ THIRTEEN ❧

Inside the Music Publishing Company

Publishing companies come in all sizes. As you will see in the coming chapters, it is possible to run a small publishing operation all by yourself. Slightly larger companies may need anywhere from three to twelve people, while a major publishing enterprise may have scores of employees located around the world.

In recent years, because so many of the large publishing companies have merged, there are fewer companies that fall into the category of the major music publisher. Most publishing companies today are of the smaller variety, consisting of a handful of employees. No matter what size the company is, there are certain functions that a publishing enterprise must undertake to be fully operational. These functions are divided up into several departments.

1. Creative
2. Licensing
3. Copyright
4. Legal and Business Affairs
5. Print
6. International
7. Royalty
8. Accounting

Overseeing this group of departments is the director of operations. This person's actual title may differ from company to company. Sometimes the person in this position is called the general manager or the vice president of administration, while in other companies this person is called something else entirely. Whatever the title, the duties are essentially the same. In extremely large publishing companies, there may even be more than one director of operations. In fact, each department may have a director (a vice president of creative affairs, for example) who reports to the president or chief executive officer. Sometimes, instead of a single chief executive who dictates all of the major decisions to his subordinates, there are two or three top executives in the company who are on near-equal ground and who make group decisions. How a publishing company is managed depends on the overall size and structure of the organization. Simply put, most publishing companies have one person (or a group of persons) that oversees the operations and that makes policy decisions.

If this all seems a bit unwieldy, it is. However, each song in the publishing company has a life of its own, and each of those songs must receive proper attention if it is to reach its full potential. Therefore, it can take many people to run a company that owns thousands of copyrights.

The Creative Department

The department primarily responsible for seeing that each song gets a fair chance of reaching that full potential is the creative department. (In some companies this department is known as the professional or A&R* department.) Depending on the size of the company, the creative department can be one person handling all of the creative duties, or several people, each responsible for his own area of specialization or group of staff songwriters.

The head of the department might be known as the creative director, the creative manager, or the VP of creative affairs. The creative director and his staff have several specific responsibilities. Among the most important are signing songs and/or staff writers and getting songs recorded.

The creative director is responsible for being able to "hear" a songwriter's talent or a song's hit potential. Most creative directors want to find writers they can work with over a long period of time. A dependable songwriter who continually creates commercial songs is an extremely important asset who can help create a very valuable catalog for a company.

Aside from finding talented writers, it is often the creative director's job to negotiate exclusive staff writer deals on behalf of the publishing company. Like a hip used-car salesman, the creative director has to play both ends of the deal—fighting for the writer to get the most advance money and the best splits he can, yet remaining a company man and letting the writer know when he's gotten the best deal he's going to get. After these preliminary discussions between the creative director and the songwriter, the attorneys for the publishing company and the songwriter work out the details of the staff writer contract.

Once a staff writer is on board, it's the job of the creative director (or a member of the creative staff) to nurture the songwriter's talent through encouragement, praise, enthusiasm, and anything else it takes to get the writer to create the kind of material the creative department is looking for. Frequently the writer will be teamed up with others (sometimes other staff writers) in an attempt to find the formula that results in the best songs.

The song plugger is another member of the creative department and has an extremely important role. As you may recall from chapter one, song plugging goes all the way back to the days before Tin Pan Alley. The song plugger is obligated to know everybody in the entertainment business who might possibly be the link to getting a song used or recorded. It is the plugger's job to see that songs belonging to the publishing company are brought to the attention of record company A&R personnel, artists' lawyers, managers, record producers, or the artists themselves.

---

*A&R stands for *artists and repertoire* (jokingly known in some music business circles as *airplanes and restaurants*). The A&R person at a record company is responsible for finding and signing artists to the record label. The A&R person at a publishing company is responsible for finding songwriter/artists, signing them to the publishing company, and then trying to get an A&R person at a record company to sign that songwriter/artist to the record company's label.

Due to the enormous success of soundtracks to films such as *O Brother, Where Art Thou?* and earlier films like *The Bodyguard, Forrest Gump, Purple Rain, Dirty Dancing*, and *Saturday Night Fever*, many creative departments have staff members who specialize in developing contacts within the film industry, making every effort to see that songs from their catalog get included in movies that use a lot of pop, rock, rap, hip-hop, R&B, or country songs in their soundtracks. They do the same for television shows that feature popular music.

Another function of the creative department is to find songwriter/performers with whom development deals can be made. Although some publishing companies refer to their entire creative staff as the A&R department, other companies have specific members of the creative staff who are assigned the A&R title. It is the A&R person's job to frequent nightclubs and other places in search of acts with original material who can be signed to the publishing company. Once the act is signed, artist demos (or, sometimes, finished masters) are made and shopped to record companies in an effort to acquire recording contracts for the songwriter/performers.

The Licensing Department

The licensing department is responsible for negotiating and issuing licenses, including mechanical, synchronization, and new media licenses. Although—depending on how a particular publishing company is set up—issuing mechanical licenses can be the domain of either the licensing department or the copyright department, synchronization and new media licenses definitely fall under the purview of the licensing department. In a really large publishing company, there might be one person in charge of movie licensing, another responsible for commercial licensing, another who handles television licenses, and a fourth person who just does new media licensing.

If the publishing company is aggressive about licensing, there may even be people on staff in the creative or licensing departments who are responsible for going out and drumming up business by approaching advertising agencies. For instance, the publisher of "I Love My Dog" might send out a member of the licensing or creative department to all of the advertising agencies who have dog food manufacturers as clients. It is that person's job to try to convince the ad agencies to sell their clients on the idea of "I Love My Dog" as the perfect song for their next commercial.

As you can see, the primary goal of every publisher is to exploit the songs in his catalog, so the jobs of the creative department and the licensing department can sometimes overlap in pursuit of that goal.

The producers or directors of most television shows, commercials, and films decide what songs they want to use without any outside help from a music publisher. If the publishing company is large enough, usually all the licensing department has to do is sit back and wait for the phone to ring, the fax to come in, or the e-mail to arrive. When a call comes in from an ad agency, a music clearance organization, a film company, or the production company of a television show, it is the job of the licensing department to negotiate the fee for the use of the song. Once the fee has been negotiated, a license is sent out that covers the fee, terms, and options that have been agreed upon.

The licensing department also usually handles grand rights usages. If a song or songs in the

The Music Publishing Capitals: L.A., N.Y.C., and Nashville

Although there are music publishing companies throughout the United States, the three undisputed music capitals in this country are Los Angeles, New York City, and Nashville. Every publishing company in these three cities has its own way of conducting business, but the publishers in each of the music capitals seem to have traits indigenous to their home city.

Steve Day has been an executive in the Nashville music industry for more than two decades. He points out, "Many people . . . have made the observation that Nashville is now the Tin Pan Alley that New York once was. Nashville is now the 'Brill Building,' if you will. It's become a mecca for songwriters."

New York and Los Angeles, in general, seem to have a different approach to the publishing business than Nashville has. Greg Sowders, Senior Vice President of A&R for Warner/Chappell Music in Los Angeles, says the tendency in New York and L.A. is to sign writer/performers:

L.A. and New York are mostly about signing artist/writers and producer/writers, as opposed to regular, old-fashioned songwriters. This is especially true with the R&B scene on both coasts, where it seems like artists and publishers alike get their songs from producer/writers.

I don't really find wild differences between L.A. and New York, except that the film and TV scene is more favorable to L.A., whereas New York seems to be more fertile in the area of commercials because of the ad agencies there and in Chicago.

I'm based in L.A., but I work in New York a couple of weeks a year. When I go there, I see different faces, but I still do the same things I do in L.A. It's when I go to Nashville that I know I'm in another world.

The art of song plugging is probably a lot healthier in Nashville than it is in L.A. or New York. It's a place where a lot of artists are still looking for material. And, it's a place where smaller publishers can exist more easily. It's not just the mega-corporations running the show there. You can be a guy who runs a catalog of twenty-five songs. If one hits, it makes the same kind of money that one of those songs signed to a major publisher makes.

Greg Sowders says that most young songwriters in New York and L.A. are offered co-publishing deals, even if they've never had a song recorded before. In Nashville, however, a songwriter signing his first deal might still have to grant as much as 100 percent of the publisher's share to an established music publisher.

However, in all three publishing capitals, once a writer is so well-established that he or she doesn't need an outside publisher at all, publishers will jump at the chance to enter into an administration deal with that writer.

catalog are going to be included in a live theatrical presentation, the licensing department will negotiate a nightly or weekly fee to be paid per song, often based on a percentage of the gross box office receipts. There are times when grand rights licenses can be so complex, the agreements are negotiated by the legal department rather than by someone in licensing.

The Copyright Department

Overlapping with the licensing department is the copyright department. It is sometimes the copyright department's job to negotiate and issue mechanical licenses. Some publishing companies have at least a dozen different types of synch licenses, but there are only a couple of types of mechanical licenses: the standard mechanical license, which can be adapted to the particular rate granted (statutory, three-quarters, etc.); and the controlled composition mechanical license. The latter license is used when an artist is bound by a controlled composition clause in his recording contract. (A controlled composition clause states that the record company will pay a reduced mechanical rate on the song titles controlled by the artist rather than by an outside publisher. For more information, see the discussion of the controlled composition clause in chapter fourteen.)

Some of the other responsibilities of the copyright department are: (1) filing various forms and documents with the Copyright Office; (2) keeping track of copyright transfers from one publishing company to another; (3) keeping the royalty and international departments apprised of new songs that have become a part of the catalog, or of old songs that have undergone a change in ownership; and (4) acting as liaison with the performing rights societies.

When a song is signed to a publishing company, or when a song is written by a staff writer, the copyright department is responsible for registering the new work with the Copyright Office. When entire catalogs are acquired (such as when one publishing company purchases another publishing company), the copyright department must notify the licensees and the royalty department where to send payments, and it must file copyright assignments with the Copyright Office.

The Legal and Business Affairs Department

Depending on the size of the publishing company, the legal and business affairs department (sometimes known as just the legal department or the business affairs department) consists of one or more lawyers and the other personnel usually associated with a law office. If the company is small- to medium-size, it might not have an in-house legal department. All of the legal work in a smaller publishing company is frequently handled by entertainment lawyers from an outside law firm, while the less complex business affairs issues are handled by someone in-house who has a good grasp of the intricacies of copyright law and business in general.

It is the job of the legal and business affairs department to keep the publishing company up-to-date on the latest changes in the copyright law, as well as on any judgments handed down that might affect the way the company conducts business. (At this particular point in music publishing history, issues regarding the use of music on the Internet have resulted in disputes regarding copyright protection in various courts both here and abroad, causing the legal and business affairs departments to be busier than ever.)

When a new publishing company is formed, the publisher wants to have single-song contracts and staff writer contracts created that are primarily in the publisher's favor. Over the years, lawyers have created many variations on the standard song contract. It is the obligation of the legal and business affairs department to be sure that each contract has the necessary clauses and legalese to fully protect the interests of the publishing company.

Once the contracts have been created, the legal and business affairs department must be prepared to let the publisher know how much leeway is advisable before a contract being negotiated will tilt away from favoring the publisher and lean toward favoring the songwriter.

The responsibilities of the legal and business affairs department include: (1) developing all of the types of contracts and licenses to be used by the publishing company; (2) working with the creative department in the negotiation of any particular writer contract; (3) defending the publishing company when lawsuits arise (or acting as liaison to the outside litigating attorneys who actually handle such cases); (4) overseeing the filing of lawsuits when there appears to be sufficient evidence that a copyright infringement has occurred (or when two publishers are claiming the same song); and (5) keeping the publishing company within legal boundaries in any given situation.

The Print Department

Like the legal department, the print department of a publishing company will be in-house only in a large publishing company. Very few publishers today have their own print departments. For the most part, today's copyright-owning publishing companies farm out their print work to print publishers who specialize in printing sheet music, folios, band and choral arrangements, and other printed editions of songs.

Whether the print department is in-house or not, it is the job of the copyright-owning publishing company to authorize the printing of music, and the job of the print department or print publisher to report to the royalty department the amount and type of printed music that has been sold.

The International Department

The duties of the international department can vary widely. As explained in chapter nine, some publishing companies own their own publishing companies outside of the United States; others have subpublishing agreements with foreign publishers. A third group maintains subpublishing deals with other domestic publishers who fit into one of the two categories mentioned above; and there are publishers who fall into other categories of foreign representation. In any of these cases, it is the responsibility of the international department to oversee the activities of the publishing catalog outside of the United States and to take whatever action is necessary to keep the international operation running smoothly.

And just as subpublishers represent the U.S. publisher abroad, the U.S. publisher frequently acts as subpublisher to foreign publishing companies. Although all of the publishing company's departments are responsible for representing the foreign publishers' catalogs, the international department usually acts as liaison between the American publisher and its foreign affiliates.

The Royalty Department

The royalty department manages the income generated through the work of all of the other departments of a publishing company. The royalty department staff is responsible for keeping track of all of the money that has come in and gone out regarding each and every song owned, co-owned, administered, or subpublished by the publisher. Then the royalty department determines how much is owed to all of the various parties who participate in the income of each song.

For example, if a song has three publishers and five writers, the royalty departments of all three publishing companies have to know who is responsible for collecting what percentage of the income and who is responsible for payment to which writers. Whatever the scenario, the royalty department generates the statements and checks that are sent out to all parties owed royalties. These statements and checks are issued semiannually, quarterly, or in whatever manner has been dictated by agreements among all of the parties involved.

The Accounting Department

Although accounting is not necessarily an in-house function (whether a publisher has an accounting department depends on the size of the company), the accounting department is another department that is necessary to almost all publishing businesses. Because of the nature of today's publishing business, it is often the accountants—along with lawyers—who rise to the top of the larger music publishing empires—probably because these larger publishing entities are public companies owned by stockholders who expect to see higher profits posted each year. Accountants noted for their excellent money-management skills can often reach top management positions in publishing companies without knowing even one of the songs in the publishing company's catalog.

The Publishing Company Scenario

Rover Doberman has written a song called "Doghouse Blues." He takes it to Snoop Beagle Music Publishing Company because he knows how successful the company was with their last hit, "I Love My Dog."

A member of the creative department listens to the song and thinks it has great potential, although a few of the lines are a little weak and the melody could use a bit more variation.

The creative department staff member plays "Doghouse Blues" for the creative director. The creative director agrees that the song is very good but needs a little work. Since Rover doesn't have any more material prepared to play for the publishing company and no previous hits, the creative director decides to offer Rover a single-song contract rather than a staff writer deal.

"I'd like to sign your song," he tells Rover, "but I think it needs some work. I'd like to let one of our staff writers take a crack at polishing it up. Of course, that means you'll have to allow him to share writer credits and royalties with you."

"You mean the writer's share of the royalties will be split fifty-fifty?" Rover asks.

"Not necessarily. It depends on how much the song is revised. But I guarantee you'll retain at least 50 percent of the writer's share."

Rover thinks for a moment and says, "Have the contract drawn up and sent to my lawyer."

The creative director asks the legal and business affairs department to issue the company's standard single-song contract with an additional clause stating that there will be a co-writer on the song who will receive no more than 50 percent of the writer's share of royalties resulting from income earned on the composition.

Once the contract has been drawn up, it is sent to Rover's lawyer. The lawyer notes several changes he would like to see made in the agreement. Most of them are minor, but when hecomes to the clause about the co-writer, he calls Rover and says, "I think it would be in your best interest to insist that the co-writer receive only 25 percent of the writer's share unless he changes half of the song, in which case 50 percent would be acceptable." Rover agrees.

The lawyer then sends the suggested changes in the contract back to the legal and business affairs department. After consulting with the creative director, the legal and business affairs department contacts Rover's lawyer, agreeing to change the co-writer clause as he requested. Other minor points are worked out, including Rover's approval of the final version of the song.

Once Rover has signed the contract, the creative director turns Rover's song over to a staff writer named Fido Dachshund. Fido punches up a few of the lyrics, makes a slight revision to the chord structure, and—with Rover's approval—the song is finished.

> The song plugger is obligated to know everybody in the entertainment business who might possibly be the link to getting a song used or recorded.

A member of the creative department takes Rover, Fido, and a group of musicians into a recording studio, where a demo of the song is made. CDs and lead sheets of the demo are thengiven to the creative and copyright departments. The creative department staff begins discussing who might be the right act to cut the tune, while a member of the copyright department fills out a Form PA and sends it to the Copyright Office for registration.

A few weeks later, a member of the creative department finds out that a band called Spot and His 103 Dalmatians are in the studio and are in need of just one more song to finish their current album. He plays "Doghouse Blues" for the group, and they agree to record it.

A short while later, the record company for Spot and His 103 Dalmatians requests a mechanical license for "Doghouse Blues." The licensing department (or copyright department, depending on the company's structure) issues the license or has it issued by the Harry Fox Agency, and the album is released.

The record company feels "Doghouse Blues" has hit potential, so the song is released as a single (at which point another mechanical license is issued for the single). As the record begins to move up the charts, the publishing company's print department jumps into action and prints sheet music of "Doghouse Blues" with a photo of Spot and His 103 Dalmatians on the cover (a practice dating back to the earliest days of publishing).

Meanwhile, the international department has notified the publishing company's subpublishers that "Doghouse Blues" has been added to the catalog and that a recording of the song has been released in the United States. At this point, each of the subpublishers' various departments will go into action, just as the U.S. publisher did when the song was signed. If there are no plans for the American recording to be released in a particular subpublisher's territory, that subpublisher's creative department will go to work attempting to get a cover of "Doghouse Blues" (or an adaptation or translation of the song) for that territory.

> The producers or directors of most television shows, commercials, and films decide what songs they want to use without any outside help from a music publisher.

Soon royalties are coming into the publishing company from the record company, foreign sources, and the performing rights society. Also, the print department (or the outside print publisher) reports to the royalty department on the amount of sheet music sold.

The royalty department then determines the amount of royalties due to Rover and Fido based on the song contract. Rover and Fido, of course, get their domestic and foreign performance royalties directly from their performing rights society, but are paid their share of mechanical, print, and other foreign royalties by the royalty department of the publishing company.

Now that the song is a hit, it's the job of the creative department and the licensing department to see to it that the song reaches its full potential. This means finding new uses for the song after it has run its course on the pop charts. Commercials, movies, and television shows are among the most obvious outlets for "Doghouse Blues" if the publisher wants it to continue to have a long, healthy life.

However, overly extensive use of a song (referred to in the music business as overexposure) can sometimes be dangerous to a copyright. A publisher must be selective in determining which uses to allow. All of us, at one time or another, have grown extremely tired of songs played too often or used in an offensive manner. (How many times have you seen one of your favorite songs used in a commercial for toilet paper or a product that helps unclog stuffed nasal passages—or worse?)

A great song that isn't overexposed throughout the years can keep coming back to be a hit again and again. The classic song "Stand by Me" was a top-twenty-five hit in 1961, 1967, 1970, 1975, 1980, 1986, and again in 1998. During that thirty-seven-year period, the song was also used in a Broadway show, as the title and theme song of a movie, and in a handful of commercials. If the publisher had chosen to allow *every* film, television show, and (especially) commercial request that came in over the years to be granted, we might all be pretty tired of the tune by now.

Granted, there aren't too many songs great enough to achieve the success of "Stand by Me," but a publisher who is careful about the manner in which a copyright is handled can actually earn millions of dollars during the time he owns and controls it.

FOURTEEN

Starting Your Own Company

Music publishing is a business. If you have a relatively good head for business—or even a marginally good head for business—you will want to seriously consider having your own publishing company at some point in your songwriting career (preferably sooner rather than later). It's hard for me to understand why a songwriter would want to give 100 percent of the publisher's share of his song to an outside publisher when some, most, or even all of the publisher's share could belong to the songwriter's own publishing company.

However, I've almost always been on the business end of the music business, so I can't claim to know what it's like to actually be a professional songwriter and have a songwriter's point of view of music publishing. But I have known an awful lot of songwriters over the years—almost all of whom ended up forming their own publishing companies—and I can safely say that I've yet to find a single songwriter who regretted the decision to step into the business world.

Since you've made it all the way to chapter fourteen of this book, it's apparent that you are interested enough in publishing that you will probably want to have your own publishing company some day—if not at the beginning of your career, then as soon as possible after the hits start coming.

The bottom line is this: If you write a song and allow me to be your sole publisher, I will get half of all the royalties your song earns. If you allow me to co-publish a song with your publishing company, and the publisher's share is split fifty-fifty between our companies, then I will get 25 percent of all the income your song makes. If you want me to administer your publishing company at a rate of 15 percent of the gross income, then I will get 15 percent of all of the royalties for the duration of the administration agreement.

If you have your own publishing company and you administer that company yourself, then I will get nothing and you will get 100 percent of the publisher's share and 100 percent of the songwriter's share (assuming, of course, that you wrote the song by yourself). However, there is a lot of work involved in administering a publishing company, and enough expenses involved that you may be better off allowing someone else to administer your company for you.

Unless your attitude is that you just don't want to be bothered with business details at all, the time will come when you should form your own publishing company, even if you still split your songs with another publisher or rely on outside administration. After all, a professional administrator or an administering co-publisher will take care of most of the important publishing business for you, leaving you more time to write songs. And whatever the administrator's fee or co-publisher's percentage may be, you won't have as much money coming out of your pocket as you would if you signed all of the publishing away to an outside company.

As I said earlier, I have known a lot of songwriters and have met very few successful ones who didn't have a publishing company of their own. Granted, many of these songwriters' biggest hits were signed away to outside publishers early in their careers. It was usually this "live and learn" aspect of their lives that caused them eventually to start their own companies in the first place.

Jerry Leiber and Mike Stoller—inductees into both the Rock and Roll Hall of Fame and the Songwriters Hall of Fame—are among the most successful songwriting teams of all time. They learned early on the importance of owning their own publishing company. One of Leiber and Stoller's first hits was the original recording of "Hound Dog" by Big Mama Thornton. (Her version predated Elvis's by three years.) Mike Stoller recalls, "We had this number-one hit by Big Mama Thornton on Peacock Records, but after resolving some problems in getting songwriter royalties from Don Robey—who owned the record label and the publishing rights to 'Hound Dog'—he left town and stopped payment on the check. Not getting paid on a million-selling record sparked the idea that we could have our own publishing company. Simply, the idea was that Jerry and I shouldn't end up being screwed out of our royalties again."

Rupert Holmes is one successful writer who determined that self-publishing was right for him. "I had a record deal and I was producing my own albums," he says. "I didn't know anyone who was going to do anything great for my songs that I couldn't do myself. It made more sense for me to keep the publishing until someone could show me that it made more sense for *them* to acquire the publishing. And the only time it made more sense was when a publisher offered to give me a great deal of money and split the publishing so that I got to keep half of it. For half of the publishing, they would also do the administration, which was a lot of paperwork I didn't want to do myself."

Songwriter and record producer Kevin Bowe shares the opinion that writers should publish their own songs:

> *There are many legitimate business reasons for starting your own publishing company, but I believe that emotionally it is a good thing to do as well. The more you can put yourself in the position of being responsible for your own career, the better off you'll be. Almost every writer I've ever met has been frustrated by their publisher promising to do things that didn't get done. After all, if you look realistically at any publishing deal, the bottom line is this: If the songs don't get cut because the writer does a bad job—the writer gets dropped. If the songs don't get cut because the publisher does a bad job—the writer gets dropped! Although it's a little more work, I think most writers are better off—if they can make it without the advance—to take care of their own publishing.*
>
> *In my case, after three publishing deals in which I was responsible for generating much more money than any of my publishers were, I started running all my new songs solely through my own publishing company. I hired an administrator and several song pluggers, and the company is now generating serious revenue.*

If you are still doubtful about the importance of having your own company, find a successful songwriter who doesn't own or co-own the publishing on her biggest hit and ask her if she wishes she had the publishing on that song, or if she's happy about having it published by an outside company—particularly if that outside company now owns hundreds of thousands of other copyrights.

The Big Catch-22

If you've never had a song recorded, it may seem there is a major catch-22 involved in forming your own publishing company. Almost all of us who applied for our very first job sat across the desk from a prospective employer who told us, "You can't get a job without some experience," to which we replied, "But how can I have had any experience if I haven't had a job before?" Right now you might be thinking, *How can I have a publishing company if I don't have a song recorded? And if I'm going to have a song recorded, how is that possible without going to an outside publisher?*

As I said before, you, as a songwriter, always have options. A couple of those major options are co-publishing your song with an established publisher or allowing an outside publisher or independent administrator to administer your publishing company for you.

I'll be the first to admit that, at the beginning of your songwriting career, it might be very difficult to get your first song cut by a major artist on a major label and still walk away with 100 percent of the publishing. However, it's not impossible. If your song is good enough, and an artist wants to record it badly enough, you're in a powerful position.

Should you by some stroke of luck reach that position, you might be tempted with a single-song agreement offering a massive advance against future royalties; a staff writer deal; a co-publishing agreement; or a host of other wonderful things that might seem impossible to pass up. But that big advance might turn out to be no more than a loan of a sum of money that you would be entitled to anyway should your song become a hit; you might not want to be tied down to a staff writer deal; and a co-publishing agreement will still usually take away more than an administrator's fee would.

"But wait," you say. "How will my song get into the hands of that major artist without a publisher?" The answer is: *You* will be the publisher. Acting as your own music publisher cuts out the middleman that many songwriters wrongly believe is an absolute requisite to becoming a successful songwriter. Of course, I don't want to imply that going out and getting your own songs recorded by superstars (or anyone else) is a simple task. In fact, one of the main advantages of being signed to an established publishing company is having access to the creative department's contacts in the recording and film industries. I'm only trying to point out that, should you begin to develop contacts in those industries, you might find yourself in a position to plug your songs and not have to sign away part or all of the publishing.

The Songwriter/Performer

If you sign a recording contract (or your band does), it is almost essential that you have your own publishing company. Why sign a publishing agreement if you are the one responsible for getting your songs recorded in the first place?

One of the main functions of a publisher is to exploit your songs. If you are a recording artist, you are exploiting your own songs when you record them yourself. If your songs are signed to an outside publisher, you don't really want her to be trying to get your songs cut by other acts right away. If she does, you may find yourself competing against another act who's trying to get a hit with the song you wish to take up the charts yourself. So, in this case, what's the point of having an outside publisher? Do you really need her to collect your money and keep part of it, when you've done all the legwork necessary to get the songs cut?

Even worse is the idea of signing a publishing agreement with a publishing company affiliated with the record company. The main function of a record company is to make and sell records. In many cases, their publishing company is merely collecting money from the record company across town, or across the hall (or across the room).

THE CONTROLLED COMPOSITION CLAUSE

Songwriter/performers who control the publishing of their own songs avoid losing the publisher's share of royalties from those songs, but they must watch out for another potential drain on royalties: the *controlled composition* clause. Controlled compositions are songs owned and controlled by the songwriter/performer. Generally this means songs written by the songwriter/performer and not signed to an outside publisher. A controlled composition clause in the recording contract of a songwriter/performer states that the record company will pay a reduced rate on the titles controlled by the artist.

This means that if a song on the album is written by an outside party, that song will earn more for the outside party than a song written by the recording artist will earn the artist as a songwriter. The only exception to this rule is when the publisher of an outside song—usually in an effort to curry favor with the record label—agrees to go along with the terms of the controlled composition clause. (Of course, this isn't particularly helpful to the outside songwriter, since his or her royalties will be diminished as well.) Although the songwriter/performer may find it difficult (or near impossible) to achieve, it is in her best interest to have any controlled composition clause removed from her contract before signing with a record company.

Some controlled composition clauses allow the record company to pay a reduced mechanical rate on a maximum number of songs in an album. (In music business parlance, this maximum number of songs is known as the *cap*.) In other words, if the clause says that the record company will pay 75 percent of the statutory rate on a cap of twelve songs, the artist may have to take a serious cut in songwriter pay if any outside (noncontrolled) songs are included on the CD.

Here's how it would work: Joe is a singer/songwriter who has a controlled composition clause in his contract that says the record company will pay 75 percent of stat (the statutory rate) with the cap at twelve songs. Joe records six songs he wrote himself and six songs written by other songwriters. Unfortunately for Joe, the publishers of the six outside songs refuse to grant a reduced rate for the use of their songs.

The statutory rate is 8.5 cents, but the maximum amount the record company will agree to pay for each of the songs on the album is 6.375 cents (a total of 76.5 cents for the twelve songs). Meanwhile, the outside publishers are demanding 8.5 cents for each of their songs, for a total of 51 cents for their six songs. This means Joe is only going to receive 25.5 cents for his own six songs (76.5 cents minus 51 cents)—the equivalent of only 4.25 cents per song.

To carry this concept another step, imagine an album of twelve songs filled with samples. On top of the controlled composition that allows the artist to receive only 75 percent of the statutory rate on twelve songs, there are all the outside songs to be considered which were sampled in the first place. It is entirely conceivable that the sampled songs could not only use up the entire allowance for mechanical royalties that the record company has granted to the artist, but also cut into the performer's artist royalties.

For example, let's say that an artist writes and records twelve new songs, but samples twenty-four other songs over the course of those twelve. (To keep this simple, we'll say that each of the artist's new songs includes two samples of outside songs.) Then let's say that all of the publishers of those twenty-four outside songs demand that their share of the new songs the artist created be 50 percent of the mechanical royalties. At this point, assuming the outside publishers agree to be bound by the artist's controlled composition clause, each of the artist's new songs now has an effective mechanical royalty of zero (each song contains two samples, and each sample earns its publisher 50 percent of the mechanical royalties, for a total of 100 percent).

But what happens if all twenty-four publishers want to charge the statutory rate for their 50 percent? Each outside publisher will get 4.25 cents per album, and their total mechanical royalties for the album will be $1.02 (4.25 cents times twenty-four). Since the record company will only pay a total of 76.5 cents in mechanical royalties for the album, the artist is suddenly in the hole for 25.5 cents ($1.02 minus 76.5 cents). Let's hope he's getting a good royalty as an artist, or this album is going to cost him money every time he sells a copy!

This scenario might be an exaggeration, but only a slight one. Imagine if the artist had a controlled composition clause with a cap of twelve songs, but decided to record sixteen songs, with each track containing a couple of samples. Hopefully, for the sake of the artist, the outside publishers won't ask for such high percentages. Otherwise, that artist will need to sell a lot of concert tickets and T-shirts just to make ends meet.

When Should You Yield to Temptation?

By now I may have convinced you that you should strongly consider self-publishing. But, in the music business, there are very few absolutes. If self-publishing seems such an obvious route to take, why doesn't everyone start her own publishing company and publish 100 percent of everything she writes?

Some songwriters sign with music publishing companies because they prefer not to deal with the business aspect of music publishing. This reason isn't good enough by itself, however, because the business aspect of songwriting is impossible to avoid entirely. Successful songwriting generates a great deal of business-related activities—unless you write for the sheer pleasure of writing, with no intention of having your songs recorded. For instance, you will need to learn how to read royalty statements. You will have to hire an accountant and a lawyer. The accountant will require you to keep track of your expenses and receipts, while your lawyer will take up your time (while you pay for hers) advising you about contracts and other legal details of the songwriting life. There is always much paperwork to do and much time to be consumed by things that aren't nearly as creative or enjoyable as songwriting itself. You can't avoid business-related activities entirely by signing with a music publisher.

But there are other strong reasons for going with an outside publisher. If a publisher hears your song and offers you a large advance, she is offering you something your own publishing company can't. The advance is why many songwriters decide to throw the concept of self-publishing out the window.

If a publisher tells you that Britney Superseller is her best friend and that Ms. Superseller is in the studio right now but will only record your song if the publisher delivers it to her by hand (and, by the way, here's a $50,000 advance), and you've never had a song recorded by anybody before—you may find your hand has separated itself from the rest of your body and has signed on the dotted line without your being able to stop it.

Then there is the matter of the record deal. If you are a songwriter/performer and you have been turned down by several record companies, you might be offered a recording contract by a label if—and only if—you agree to sign a publishing or co-publishing deal with the record label's sister publishing company.

It's not always easy (and sometimes it might not even be wise) to insist on controlling 100 percent of the publishing on every song you write. Every case is different, and your decision should depend on the situation and circumstances. One thing is certain, though: You don't want to give away the publishing if you don't have to. So, it's best to be ready for the moment when luck is on your side—when a record producer you know is in the studio and desperate for one more song, or when it turns out that the drunk guy you drove home from a bar last night is actually a major recording artist who now owes you his life and is looking for new songs for his next album.

Whatever the scenario, if you can keep some or all of the publishing in a particular situation, you should be prepared to do so—if not by already having your own company, then at least by having the knowledge necessary to set up a publishing company.

You may wonder why, if I'm so gung ho about self-publishing, I have written the first chapters of this book. One reason is fairly obvious: You, like most songwriters (especially the nonper-forming type), are probably going to find yourself dealing with outside publishers for some time as a necessary means of achieving success. A staff writer earning a thousand dollars or more a week as an advance against future royalties can live comfortably, with a feeling of security. Also, if you find yourself facing an offer too good to refuse, you should know from what you've learned in this book what some of your options are. Another reason I've written so much about working with music publishers is to give you the kind of knowledge that I hope will be of help to you if you set up your own company.

The information that follows should provide a starting point for learning how to form and run your own company. I have even tried to give you pointers on some of the aspects of handling your own administration, if you should be so inclined.

Setting Up Shop

Becoming a music publisher doesn't have to be terribly difficult or expensive. Unlike busi-nesses that require the actual manufacturing of a product, music publishing is largely a business of intangibles. But, like all businesses, your publishing company has to exist somewhere. I would recommend that you begin with that basic tool of most small businesses—the kitchen table. If you're lucky enough to have a spare room in your house or apartment, that's a fine workstation too.

There are generally three business structures in this country: the sole proprietorship, the partnership, and the corporation. Once you have made the decision to form your own publishing company, you should speak with a lawyer and/or an accountant about which of these three types of business arrangements makes the most sense for you from a legal and financial standpoint.

The most common form of small business is the sole proprietorship. If you want to start your company on a small scale, the sole proprietorship is usually the best avenue to take—at least at the beginning. However, everyone's financial circumstances are different, so you really should speak to an attorney or an accountant you trust so that she can let you know if your particular financial status would make forming a partnership or corporation more appropriate for you.

> One thing is certain, though: You don't want to give away the publishing if you don't have to.

To set up a sole proprietorship in most parts of thecountry, you must file a DBA form at your city hall or county clerk's office (DBA stands for "doing business as"). You can find standard DBA forms at almost any stationery store or on the Internet. One of the purposes of filing a DBA form is to officially inform your local government of the name of your business venture. Coming up with a name for your publishing company is an important step in becoming a publisher. Before you can choose a name, you will have to decide which performing rights society your company is going to be affiliated with. If you are already affiliated with a society as a songwriter, your publishing company must be affiliated with the same society.

Assuming you are not already affiliated with a performing rights society as a songwriter, the decision of which society you affiliate with as a writer and self-publisher should not be made lightly. You've read about all three organizations (ASCAP, BMI, and SESAC) in this book. If you haven't already made contact with any of the societies at this point in your career, now is the time. Write, e-mail, or call all three societies and ask them to send you information about their organizations, as well as applications for writer and publisher membership. Read the literature, then talk to other affiliated songwriters or publishers you know and get their opinions on the societies they belong to. All three societies have informative Web sites that provide a wealth of information about how they operate.

I would also strongly urge you to talk to representatives of each society on the phone. Are they friendly? Are they helpful? Do they sound like they're interested in having you affiliated with them? Once you've done your preliminary research, call them all back again. Can you get them on the phone right away? If not, do they return your calls promptly? The reason I'm putting an emphasis on this aspect of your business is that your performance royalty income is extremely important. If you have questions about whether you are being paid properly by your performing rights society, you don't want to have to wait days, weeks, or months for an answer.

Having run several publishing companies, I have dealt with both BMI and ASCAP frequently.

Some of the companies I have run have had several hundred songwriters signed to them. On more than one occasion, I've discovered that an outside songwriter with the same name as one of my writers was getting money that was supposed to be going to my writer. I've also had cases in which the songwriters' percentages (for songs with two or more writers) were being split improperly. On the publishing end, I've dealt with situations in which royalties due for a song transferred to one of my publishing companies were still being paid to the previous publisher. The number of things that can go wrong in the publishing business is almost unbelievable.

I discovered a long time ago that the only way to get these problems corrected is to make contacts at the societies and hound them until things get fixed. Since you will be starting from scratch and operating on a small level at the beginning, you're not as likely to encounter the same kinds of problems as would a publisher with thousands of copyrights. However, it's good to make those initial contacts and find out who you will be best able to work with before you lock yourself in to a society for an extended period of time.

Once you have decided which society is good enough (and fortunate enough) to be the performing rights society for you and your publishing company, you will have to fill out the songwriter and publisher affiliation applications. It is at this point that you will have to pick a name for your company (plus a few options, in case the name you've chosen is already in use or is too similar to another publishing company's name). There are thousands of music publishing companies in the world. The name of yours has to be completely unique, so don't be surprised if it takes a while to come up with a name somebody hasn't already thought of.

The performing rights society will check the names of all other existing publishing companies and will inform you which of your name choices is available. If you've come up with the perfect name for your company and you're anxious to get it on the books, you might want to call your contact at the performing rights society you've chosen and see if that name is available even before you fill out the publisher affiliation application. If it is, ask them to reserve the name for you. Remember that your company name is going to represent *you*, so choose something that is appropriate and that will look good on your stationery, business cards, and Web site, and in small type on CDs, sheet music, etc. Once your name has been approved, it's time to fill out your DBA form and file your business name in the manner required by your local government.

You should also check with your bank to find out what information it requires for your business checking account. Once you have a company name, a bank account in your company name, and a performing rights society affiliation, you're officially in business. Your state or county may require more on your part (especially in the area of business taxes), and your accountant or lawyer will be able to provide you with more information about that topic.

The Company Image

Your music publishing company will need to have a professional image. Since much of your business will involve correspondence, your stationery should complement that image. A sheet of plain white paper won't do. Even though most of your correspondence will probably be via e-mail and fax, you're still going to need professional-looking letterhead and envelopes from time to time, whether you create them on your computer or have them printed up for you by your local copy shop or stationer.

You might want to start by looking at the stationery of other publishing companies. If you've sent CDs out to publishers and have gotten rejection letters back (and if you didn't throw them out in a fit of anger), take a look at them now. Most publishers' stationery I've seen looks pretty conservative. But if most of your songs are novelty tunes, you might want to create stationery more consistent with the nature of your catalog. Just keep in mind that your stationery and business cards are representing you and the songs in your publishing company, as is your company name. The information on your letterhead should include your company name, address, phone and fax numbers, and e-mail address.

Your Publishing Office

By day I work in a large office with a high-backed black leather chair, a dramatic glass-top desk, gold and platinum albums on one wall, original artwork on another, and a handmade wall unit that holds all of my audio equipment. The wall behind my desk is a giant window that faces the Hollywood Hills. Outside my office is a large waiting room where a receptionist sits, keeping an eye on who's coming in and going out all day. The office is on Sunset Boulevard in Los Angeles, in the heart of the music industry of that city. Overall, it's a pretty impressive setup.

By night, however, if I'm not out attending one of the many music industry functions that take place pretty frequently in this town, I work in a spare room in my house. There are no gold records or expensive paintings in this room. Since writers don't have frequent visitors to their places of business, I'm not out to impress anyone with my workspace.

As a self-publisher, you don't need to impress anyone with a fancy office. Most of your work will be done on the phone, via e-mail, over a fax machine, through regular old-fashioned mail, or in person. But people won't be coming to see you—you'll be going to them. Always keep in mind that you are running a small home business that should remain small until enough money comes rolling in to justify an actual office with a secretary, a high-backed leather chair, and all of those other accoutrements that come with a large, successful enterprise.

So, what will your home office need and how much expense will be involved? You probably already have much of what you need. If you've been sending your songs out to publishers, then you've been printing copies of your lyrics on your computer. Two more items essential to your operation are a telephone and an answering machine. Along with your written correspondence, your phone is your contact to the outside world. You will need an answering machine or voice mail service because you can't possibly be where your phone is at all times. Most likely you have school or a day job that will keep you away from your phone when important calls are coming in. If you have a cell phone, you could use it as your business phone. (In that case, you *can* be where your phone is all the time, but you will still need a voice mail account on your cell phone just in case. Most cell phone plans include voice mail.) Or, you can include your cell phone number as part of your outgoing message on your home answering machine (or voice mail service) so people who need to can reach you right away.

One other thought about answering machines: Make your outgoing message as brief and professional as you can. If someone is taking the time to call your place of business, he doesn't want to sit through bad jokes, thirty seconds of your latest composition, or anything else that distracts from the reason he is calling you. The only exception to this advice is if your image is off-the-wall in the first place. If all you write are hilarious novelty tunes, feel free to have a field day with your answering machine message. If you deal only in serious ballads, my advice is to stick to the basics. I realize this may seem like a small point to dwell on, but more than one person has missed out on a serious opportunity whenI hung up on thirty seconds of answering-machine gibberish that I didn't have time to listen to.

Since you're a songwriter, your remaining major purchase—whatever device you choose to record your songs with—is probably already in your home. If you have your own home recording studio and a CD burner, you've got everything you need in the way of recording equipment— at least until the next wave of technology makes your current equipment outdated.

When you are beginning a small publishing company, you have to keep in mind that professional-sounding demos are very important. There are professional publishers all around you using the latest technologies available. When I speak at songwriting seminars and workshops, I always remind those in attendance that they are not only competing against the other songwriters at their level, they are also competing against the person who wrote the song sitting at the top of the various *Billboard* charts this week.

> When you are beginning a small publishing company, you have to keep in mind that professional-sounding demos are very important.

The same applies to you as a publisher. You're in competition with Warner/Chappell, EMI, Universal, Sony/ATV, and every other large and small publisher in the business today. You're even in competition with me! So, although your publishing empire might be in one corner of your bedroom, you have to give the outward appearance of being a professional enterprise.

One of your best options for establishing a professional presence in the worldwide marketplace is creating a Web site for your company. Granted, you don't want to spend the kind of fortune on yours that many large publishers have on theirs. However, you might want to seriously consider having an inexpensive—but professional-looking—page or two on the Internet. Even if the site contains just your company name and contact information—and perhaps a few audio files of some of your songs—at least you'll have a Web address to give people if they should ask. The ability to e-mail audio files of your songs is invaluable. It's quicker, easier, and cheaper than sending CDs by messenger or through the post office or a shipping company.

One more essential item for your publishing company is a subscription to *Billboard*, the most popular trade journal in the music business. The subscription rate is pretty high, so be prepared to lay out some serious money. If you have a songwriting partner or a friend who's in need of a subscription as well, perhaps the two of you can subscribe to it together. *Billboard* will provide you with the news and information you need to make contacts, to see what acts are on the charts, to find out the latest changes in the publishing business, etc. *Hits* magazine is another trade publication with a large following. *Hits* also has one of the most entertaining Web sites in the entertainment business (HitsDailyDouble.com).

Before we discuss the business aspects of operating a small-scale publishing company, let's review everything you're going to need to get started.

1. First, you'll require a space to operate in. In the beginning, that space can be the size of a kitchen table or a desk.

2. Next you'll need to find out what type of business structure is best for you: a sole proprietorship, a partnership, or a corporation.

3. Then you will need to create a name for your company (with a few options in case your first choice is already taken).

4. Once you have chosen your name, you will need to apply for affiliation with the performing rights society that you have decided upon—a decision you shouldn't make until you've done your own research and have found the society that works best for you.

5. Once your name has been approved by the performing rights society, you must file the documents required by your local government to set up your business.

6. You will need to create (or have someone else create) your company's professional stationery and business cards.

7. For printed and e-mail correspondence (and generally keeping track of your operation), you will need a computer. You will also need a phone, a fax machine, and an answering machine or voice mail service (even if your cell phone is going to also act as your business phone).

8. You will need the latest high-quality equipment for making demos and creating recordings. The songs on your demos are the product that your business is manufacturing and selling. (I know that sounds impersonal, but it is the ultimate reality of music publishing.) Therefore, your product must be excellent if you want to compete with the other publishers who are marketing their product to the same buyers you are trying to reach.

9. If it's in your budget, you should have a Web site so that your publishing company has a presence around the world, like other music publishers.

10. And, you'll need a subscription to *Billboard* (and possibly other trade journals) to keep you abreast of everything that's happening in the music business.

Day-to-Day Operation

As a self-publisher, you must either handle all of the departments and functions of a full-scale publishing company yourself, or hire an administrator. (The latter may not be necessary until you get a song or two recorded and released.) Since your main goal is to get your songs recorded and released, your primary function is to act as the creative director of your company. In other words, you must make contacts in the music industry and choose which of your songs goes to which contacts. If you live in or near one of the major music centers (such as New York City, Nashville, or Los Angeles), the time has come to start shoving your foot in the door by meeting artists' managers, record producers, recording artists, A&R people, booking agents, and anyone else who might be able to help you.

Everyone's experience in acquiring contacts is different, which makes it very difficult for anyone to say, "Here's the proper way to get to know people in the music business." My personal method was so strange that it would be almost impossible for anyone to duplicate (although perhaps not quite as strange as when a young Kris Kristofferson got Johnny Cash's attention by landing a helicopter on his lawn). The short version of my story goes like this: I quit my job as a small-town disk jockey; took a bus from Florence, Alabama, to New York City; and quickly began trying to figure out how I was going to survive. My first gig was as an assistant to the general manager of a well-known print publishing firm. After about a year with no movement upward in the company, I got a job in a museum called the Songwriters Hall of Fame, where I met some of the top songwriters in the business.

Not long after I went to work there, the gentleman who hired me left the organization. Since I had been his assistant (although for less than three months), the board of directors promoted me to his position. I'll be the first to admit it was pure luck.

Among other things, it was my job to coordinate the annual Songwriters Hall of Fame awards dinners. One of the board members who showed some personal interest in me told me it was important that I get to know everyone I could if I wanted to move up in the music business. At the annual awards dinners, I met an amazing array of the biggest names in the entertainment world.

As fate would have it, we lost our lease on the space where the museum was housed. When we were offered space for a small office in a building on West Fifty-Seventh Street in Manhattan, I ended up working on a floor that also contained the offices of a record company. As you might have guessed, I went to work for the record company, eventually running its affiliated publishing company. Meanwhile, I was elected to the board of directors of the Songwriters Hall of Fame, which allowed me to continue to meet more and more people in the industry at each function the Hall of Fame held.

Always realizing the importance of keeping my name and face in the public eye, I made friends with the trade press who attended the same functions I was attending. I also made friends with a photographer—who I made sure was standing nearby with camera in hand when I was chatting with Michael Douglas, Willie Nelson, Chuck Berry, Henry Mancini, Carole King, Dick Clark, and a host of others.

With a minimal amount of begging, I managed to get my photos with some of these famous people into *Billboard*, newspapers, and the occasional magazine. Since all of the people I needed to know in the music business were subscribers to *Billboard*, I managed to become a semifamiliar name and face to them.

Granted, I'm not as well known as the presidents of the major record companies (or even some of the vice presidents, for that matter), but I have made enough contacts over the years that I can get the attention of almost anyone I need to speak to or get a song to. If I don't know the record producer of a hot act I have a song for, it's almost a sure thing that I know someone who does. With a little networking, I will get the song heard.

As you can see from my own story, there is no set way to get to know the people you need to know. Just keep in mind that making contacts is not an impossible task—new songwriters and publishers are managing to get their songs cut all the time. If they can do it—and if your songs are as good as or better than theirs—then you can do it too.

Acting as the creative director of your own publishing company, you will have to learn to hustle. In case you're thinking that you'd rather not be your own publisher if it means having to be brave enough to go out and meet high-powered music executives, let me remind you that it takes an awful lot of work and effort to go out and meet music publishers. If your songs are going to be heard, you're going to have to start making contacts sooner or later.

But the question remains, how do you meet these seemingly elusive music industry types? To me, the most obvious method is to attend the various workshops and seminars where music executives are speaking.

In major music industry cities like New York, Nashville, and Los Angeles, there are seminars going on all the time that are sponsored by ASCAP, BMI, the National Academy of Popular Music, the Songwriters Guild of America, and other music organizations. Get on the phone, call these organizations,* and find out when and where their next function is taking place. Some seminars are free; others have fees attached. As a publisher, you will probably be able to write off these types of fees as business expenses (tax laws, like the Copyright Act, are always changing, so check with your accountant for details).

If you're lucky at these seminars, you might learn something about the business that you didn't already know. The main reason for being there, though, is to meet the speakers who can do you some good, as well as other music executives who might be in attendance.

Don't go to these functions unprepared. This is where your subscription to *Billboard* is worth its annual rate. Once you're signed up to attend a specific seminar and you know who the speakers will be, check through your issues of *Billboard* to see if you can get some detailed information about what these speakers have accomplished lately. Look them up on the Internet too. Does that record producer have a big hit on the charts? Did that A&R person just get a big promotion? Did that manager just sign a performer who uses outside material and sings the kind of songs you write? Get to know these people before you ever meet them in person.

Most importantly, follow up! I can't tell you the number of people who've come up to me at seminars where I've spoken, introduced themselves to me, shoved a CD in my hand, and then disappeared into the ether. Just like everybody else in the music business, I tend to be a tad busy. If somebody has given me a CD, she should call me and remind me about it. She should (nicely) encourage me to listen to it. She should try to squeeze my e-mail address out of me so she can correspond with me and keep reminding me she exists. (By the way, don't do this just to me. Do it to everybody in the business that you meet. If you're thinking this sounds obnoxious or overbearing, just remember that most of us in the industry got where we are by being obnoxious and overbearing!)

When my son was very young, he learned that the more persistent he was, the better his chances of getting what he wanted. For some reason, a lot of people seem to lose this talent as they get older. They make one phone call and then give up. Remember, when you're wearing your publishing hat, your job is to be as persistent as a kid wanting the latest toy.

---

*The addresses, phone numbers, and Web sites of some of these organizations are listed in the appendix.

Putting It All Together

If your songs are good, if you make enough contacts, if you refuse to give up, and if luck is on your side, then the day will finally come when someone somewhere will record one of your songs. At that point, you will need to either apply the information you've learned from this book to your own publishing business, or allow an outside administrator to do the detail work for you (and then your job will be to monitor the administrator's work based on all you now know).

If you should decide to try your hand at administration, you will have to put on your licensing department hat. The party releasing the initial recording of your song will require a mechanical license from you. Since this is the first recording of a particular work, the copyright law says you have the right to determine whether you want this first recording to be made and distributed, as well as the right to determine the royalty rate.

Realistically, though, unless the initial recording is so bad that you want to prevent its release, you are obviously going to give permission for the recording at the current statutory mechanical rate. (Although it is allowed by law, I'm not aware of anyone who has actually charged more than statutory.) You may even find yourself granting a reduced rate if circumstances require it. In fact, the label releasing the initial recording of your song may have agreed to do so only if you would grant a three-quarter rate, or allow yourself to be bound by the artist's controlled composition clause.

But to issue a mechanical license, you need to know how the license should read. One example of a mechanical license can be found in the appendix. If you prefer to have your licensing handled through the Harry Fox Agency, this would be the time to contact them about representing you.

When royalties are due from the record company that has released a recording of your song, you will need to keep track of the royalties you receive. If your mechanical license calls for royalty payments to be due within forty-five days of each calendar quarter, you will probably get paid on or very close to the forty-fifth day. (You probably won't get the money any earlier. Why? One of the primary ways record companies make money is by earning interest on the vast amounts of money they hold prior to making payments to artists and publishers. Record companies have historically taken full advantage of this forty-five-day clause, so there's no real reason to expect money to show up any earlier than the record company is contractually obligated to send it.)

Once the forty-five days are up, however, you should receive royalties on records sold during the preceding quarter. Assuming payment is made (and reputable record companies will usually pay on time), it's your job as the royalty department of your publishing company to make sure the amount of money received equals the number of copies reported on the statement times the mechanical rate agreed to in your mechanical license. If it is, congratulations. If it's not, it's time for you to get on the phone and contact the royalty department of the record company. If there is a discrepancy, it's your responsibility to get it corrected.

Unless you happen to be a combination songwriter/publisher/lawyer, though, you can't be your own legal department. If a record company still refuses to pay you even thirty or more days after, you most likely have grounds for a breach-of-contract suit. (If the breach is determined by the court to be material, you could then claim that the agreement is terminated and that further acts of manufacturing and distribution constitute copyright infringement.)

However, before you start accruing legal fees, it's best to decide if the money you're not being paid by the record company is substantially more than the amount of money your lawyer is going to charge to recover it. If the answer is no, make your best effort to recover the money yourself by hounding the record company and threatening legal action. You could also choose a lawyer willing to work on a contingency basis, in which case the lawyer's fee would be a percentage of the money recovered.

Once "distribution of . . . phonorecords . . . to the public by sale" has taken place, your composition qualifies as having been published. As your own copyright department, you will need to inform your performing rights society that your song has been released so that the society will be able to properly account to you.

If your song is a hit, it's likely that you will be approached by print publishers for the right to release your song in sheet music and folio form. Although you will probably be able to negotiate the basic points of the agreement (amount of advance, royalty per copy, etc.) yourself, it would be a good idea to have a lawyer look over the agreement to make suggestions or implement changes he feels are necessary.

Since the recording of your song will probably be released in foreign territories, you will need to start making subpublishing deals. Acting as your own foreign department, you will have to decide which of the subpublishing options discussed previously is best for your company. Obviously, you won't want to go around setting up your own foreign corporations, but you will need to get involved with subpublishers on some level, because serious money can be made in the international market.

This is the point at which you'll find out one of the advantages of having an e-mail account and owning a fax machine. You probably prefer not to do business in the middle of the night. While you're sleeping, your subpublisher—in another time zone halfway around the world— can be faxing or e-mailing you information about what is happening with your song there.

A hit song often prompts other types of uses, as I have pointed out in other sections of this book. It is possible you'll get calls requesting use of the song in commercials, movies, or television shows. In these situations, you will have to don your licensing department hat once again to negotiate a fair price for these uses.

As a self-publisher, then, you will at least have to be your own creative department. If you decide to delve into administration, you will have to act as the licensing, royalty, copyright, and international departments as well. The legal and print departments, of course, will be handled out-of-house by others qualified in those areas.

As more of your songs are recorded, your publishing company may find it needs a real office with a part- or full-time assistant/secretary/receptionist. If your success rate becomes high enough, you may find yourself turning into a larger publishing company, taking on additional writers and bringing in large sums of money.

On the other hand, the success of your publishing business can frequently leave you buried in business details, with little time for the more creative endeavors of being a songwriter. To avoid this situation, you can either try to keep the company small enough for you to handle alone (most likely by using an outside administrator) or hire someone to act as an in-house administrator. Before you decide to hire personnel, make sure that your company is active enough and financially successful enough to justify such expenses.

FIFTEEN

The Future of Music Publishing

Attempting to predict the future is not always a wise move—especially in print. Before I endeavor to prognosticate things to come, let's take a look back at what I hope you have learned so far from this guide to music publishing.

Music Publishing History

Music publishing is always evolving. From the industry's earliest days in this country, publishers have been forced to keep up with musical, social, and technological changes. Before the days of recordings and performance royalties, publishers reaped their profits from the printing and selling of sheet music and songbooks.

When recordings caught on with the public, publishers were in constant demand because performers and record companies were in need of new songs. The advent of motion pictures with sound also called for more songs to be created. Meanwhile, the first performing rights society in the United States was formed, allowing publishers and songwriters a new avenue by which to earn royalties for their works.

As years went by, artists began to record their own material; the publishing companies found themselves banging on record company doors, with each publisher trying to sell record company executives on the idea that their songs were better than their competitors. As the number of artists recording outside material grew ever smaller, competition among publishers grew stronger.

As a result, music publishers got into the business of artist development—selling not just a single song to the record company, but the entire artist/songwriter package to record companies rather than just trying to convince a record company A&R person of the merits of one particular song.

Although the buying and selling of publishing catalogs was nothing new, a sort of merger fever started sweeping through the publishing industry beginning in the 1980s. As one large company devoured another, the number of major publishers shrank to only a handful, making the resultant mega-publishers cumbersome while allowing smaller publishers to prosper and grow.

The Evolution of Copyright Law

The U.S. Copyright Act is the backbone of the music publishing business. Like the music publishing industry itself, it has evolved with the advance of technology and with creative expansion and diversification—although not as quickly as some might have wished.

Over the years, the life span of a copyright has increased dramatically; the addition of the right to collect royalties for public performance has, in some cases, doubled the amount of income available to many owners of active copyrights; and, by joining the Berne Convention and extending a copyright's duration to life-plus-seventy, the U.S. government has placed American copyright law on equal footing with copyright laws in countries throughout the rest of the world.

Royalties and Contracts

You have learned how publishers and songwriters can earn income from a song: through mechanical, synchronization, performance, and print royalties; through new technologies such as digital downloads; and through royalties earned from other countries via subpublishing.

We have discussed the main contract options available to you as a songwriter (single-song, exclusive or staff writer, co-publishing, and administration), and some of the main clauses included in such contracts. By this time you no doubt realize the importance of having a good entertainment lawyer when any of these types of agreements are offered to you.

Inside the Music Publisher

Next we went inside a music publishing company to discover how it functions. Although the legal, print, and accounting divisions are frequently not part of the publisher's in-house operation, a workable company must consist of creative, licensing, royalty, copyright, and international departments. Depending on the company's size, these departments may be handled by a small staff or by scores of employees around the world.

I have also shown you how it is possible to start your own music publishing company on a tight budget by operating out of your home and handling most of the publishing company departments by yourself.

It took me many years of trial and error to learn what I have written here. However, although I've saved you from more than two decades of study at the proverbial school of hard knocks, there will be much more for you to learn in the future—especially with the rapid growth going on in the world of technology. After all, you can't learn how to race in the Indianapolis 500 just by reading a driver's manual. In order to succeed in the music publishing industry, you have to slowly gain skill and knowledge, then put yourself to the test by applying what you've learned in here to the music publishing race going on out there.

The Future

When Columbia and RCA Victor introduced fine-grooved records that rotated at 33⅓ and 45 revolutions per minute, many people argued that the discs wouldn't become commercially acceptable because the general public would not only be required to pay higher prices for the records, they would have to purchase new equipment to play them on.

Despite the lesson that should have been learned from the fact that 78 rpm records quickly became passé after the introduction of these two new forms of vinyl records, just twenty years ago "experts" were challenging the commercial viability of compact discs based on essentially the same argument—that the general public wouldn't be open to the idea of purchasing new audio equipment or paying substantially more money for CDs than they had been paying for LPs. To paraphrase Santayana, those who aren't aware of earlier goofy predictions are doomed to repeat them. (To be fair, not every technological move the music industry made was an ongoing hit with the public. Although the 8-track tape was popular for a season, it was quickly replaced by the prerecorded cassette.)

In the very first edition of this book, I wrote:

> *This swift change {from the 8-track to the prerecorded cassette} by the general public was a sign that American society will not hesitate to move to a more practical, better-quality product when it is introduced and properly marketed. In the future, the music industry will continue to create new types of phonorecords. If these devices are more practical and of higher audio quality than those then available in the marketplace, the current model will be replaced in a briefer period of time than the "experts" will predict.*

In the years since I wrote those words, I have seen the quick rise and decline of the prerecorded Digital Audio Tape. The audio quality of DAT recordings may have been high, but DATs fell far short of what most consumers considered to be "more practical." Perhaps its poor sales figures can be chalked up to something as simple as the public's impression that audio tape can be broken, whereas CDs seem to be somewhat less destructible.

On the other hand, there has been an interesting influx of new technology such as various types of enhanced CDs, which have music on them just as regular CDs do, but which also include other material that can be viewed on one's computer screen.

Here's another quote from the first edition of this book:

> *I believe we are not too far away from a time when the industry will become tied into the personal computer. Although it may be a few years away, we will probably find ourselves with the capability of creating our own personalized compilations. . . . In the future, a person will be able to enter his selections on his home computer and create a tape that contains the recordings of his choice.*

Okay, so it turned out to be MP3 files rather than tape. At the time I wrote those words, the Internet was in its infancy. Less than two decades later, it's hard to remember how we managed to get anything done without it. The bottom line is, it turns out that I was right. Unfortunately, the major record labels ignored my prognostications. Once the compressed digital music file was developed, downloading recordings over the Internet became incredibly fast and easy. Because the record companies were slow to develop their own commercial Internet ventures, a host of illegal download services cropped up. Millions of dollars in potential royalty income were—and continue to be—lost.

Today, however, while there are still plenty of illegal services in operation, there are now a number of legal ones as well—the most successful to date being iTunes. The sound quality of the recordings is great, and the ease and low cost of downloading tunes and carrying them around on one's iPod has resulted in hundreds of millions of legal iTunes downloads.

So, to repeat one of my earlier predictions, *society will not hesitate to move to a more practical, better-quality product when it is introduced and properly marketed.* While the record labels are scrambling around, trying to promote CDs at exorbitant prices and DualDiscs at even more exorbitant prices, kids (and a lot of grownups) around the world are busy loading up their iPods. Talk about a product being properly marketed!

Purchasing music via the Internet is the present—and the future—of the music business. It's that simple.

I'm not trying to imply that physical stores selling recordings won't continue to exist in some form. However, it is interesting to note that, since the advent of television—and especially since the Internet explosion—Americans have been spending more and more time at home. Also, by providing recorded music directly to the consumer via iTunes and similar services, as well as by selling CDs via amazon.com and other virtual stores, record companies now have the capacity to bypass the middlemen (in this case, distributors and physical stores) and make higher profits for themselves.

Before we delve too far into the futuristic possibilities of technology, let's consider music publishing's role in the immediate years ahead. Obviously, no matter what device is used to transmit recorded music, as long as copyright law manages to keep up with technological advances and inflation, music publishers will continue to thrive. The big question is what form publishing will take in the future.

As I have said several times, the most radical change of recent vintage in the publishing world—the consolidation of several large publishers into just a few mega-publishers—has resulted from the remarkable number of mergers among the major players in the industry. When I first came up with the idea of writing this book, Warner Bros. had not yet bought Chappell & Co. Shortly after I began working on the first edition, EMI bought SBK. Then, even before I had

> I predict that in the future there will be vast new opportunities for music publishers of all sizes.

a chance to finish the second edition, Sony and ATV merged. Since then we have seen the merger of major publishers PolyGram and MCA (now jointly known as Universal), as well as the sale of smaller companies to larger ones—such as Berry Gordy's Jobete to EMI.

In the first edition of this book, I predicted that "these mergers and takeovers will continue until there are only two or three major publishing companies in the country." As it turns out, we are edging closer and closer to that day. What once were many are now only five: Warner/Chappell, EMI, Sony/ATV, BMG, and Universal.

I also predicted that these mergers would cause the industry to become very top-heavy, opening doors for dozens of smaller independent companies to compete on a more active basis. I think this, too, has come to fruition; companies such as Windswept Pacific, and Spirit Music Group have become extremely successful in recent years, even though the size of their catalogs combined can't begin to compete with the catalog of a company like Warner/Chappell. When the record industry became a game with only a handful of major players, it was very difficult for independent labels to compete for space on the charts. Publishing differs, though, since songs are required by all record labels, large and small. Also, since an independent publishing company can exist with a very low overhead, it is an easier business to finance than an independent record company.

The biggest problem the large conglomerate-type publishers now find themselves facing is the lack of personal contact with the thousands and thousands of songwriters whose songs they represent. Although smaller publishers may not be able to compete in the area of advances to staff writers, these smaller companies are able to have a more personal relationship with their writers.

Way back in 1989, Rupert Holmes saw the future this way: "The good news is that the music business will be making more money than ever. The bad news is that there will be fewer people making that money." However, as Holmes predicted, there are advantages—for some—to the big-business syndrome. "Anytime anything gets this huge and conglomerated, there are cracks in the hull of the huge corporate ship. That's where the smaller publisher is going to actually be in better shape than he was before. It's going to take smaller publishers who are willing to stick their necks out a little to make things really happen."

All these years later, it turns out that Holmes was exactly right. While the major publishing companies all seem to be run by lawyers and accountants these days, the smaller companies are mainly being run by real music men and women who got into the business to promote music rather than to constantly worry about numbers and legalese. Like crumbs from the king's table, many opportunities will continue to fall through the cracks in the major publishing companies' operations, and the smaller publishers will be there to pick them up and profit from them.

I predict that in the future there will be vast new opportunities for music publishers of all sizes. Not only will technological advances result in the creation of improved products for publishers to profit from; there will also be new avenues for publishers to take to further exploit their songs.

Finally, I truly hope that the songwriting and publishing communities will continue to gain power politically, effecting more improvements in the area of copyright protection. Greater political clout will be a necessity if the publishing industry wishes to encourage Congress to revise and strengthen copyright law to prevent the loss of untold millions of dollars through illegal copying—a process that has become easier and easier with the advent of new technology.

To Your Future

Musical fads will come and go, but there will always be a demand for good songs. As a songwriter, determining where you're going to fit in this constantly changing industry will be up to you, your talent and a heaping dose of luck.

Now that you know what music publishing is and how it functions, it's up to you to act on your newfound knowledge. If you keep up with the changes in the business, keep having faith in yourself, and keep your fingers crossed, you can succeed. Remember, thousands upon thousands of others have done it. So can you. Here's to your future!

U.S. Performing Rights Societies, Songwriters' and Publishers' Organizations, and Other Organizations of Interest

American Society of Composers, Authors, and Publishers (ASCAP)*

www.ascap.com

- One Lincoln Plaza, New York, NY 10023
  Phone: (212) 621-6000; Fax: (212) 724-9064
- 7920 West Sunset Boulevard, Third Floor
  Los Angeles, CA 90046
  Phone: (323) 883-1000; Fax: (323) 883-1049
- Two Music Square West, Nashville, TN 37203
  Phone: (615) 742-5000; Fax: (615) 742-5020

Association of Independent Music Publishers (AIMP)

www.aimp.org

- P.O. Box 69473, Los Angeles, CA 90069
  Phone: (818) 771-7301
- ℅ Burton Goldstein & Co., LLC
  156 West 56th Street, Suite 1803, New York, NY 10019
  Phone: (212) 582-7622; Fax: (212) 582-8273

Broadcast Music, Inc. (BMI)*

www.bmi.com

- 320 West 57th Street, New York, NY 10019-3790
  Phone: (212) 586-2000
  10 Music Square East, Nashville, TN 37203-4399
  Phone: (615) 401-2000
- 8730 Sunset Boulevard, Third Floor West, West Hollywood, CA 90069-2211
  Phone: (310) 659-9109

California Copyright Conference (CCC)

www.theccc.org

- P.O. Box 57962, Sherman Oaks, CA 91413
  Phone: (818) 379-3312

The Harry Fox Agency, Inc. (HFA)

www.harryfox.com

- 711 Third Avenue, New York, NY 10017
  Phone: (212) 370-5330; Fax: (646) 487-6779

Nashville Songwriters Association International (NSAI)

www.nashvillesongwriters.com

- 1701 West End Avenue, Third Floor, Nashville, TN 37203

Phone: (615) 256-3354; Fax: (615) 256-0034

National Academy of Popular Music/Songwriters Hall of Fame

www.songwritershalloffame.org

- 330 West 58th Street, Suite 411, New York, NY 10019-1827
  Phone: (212) 957-9230; Fax: (212) 957-9227

National Music Publishers' Association (NMPA)

www.nmpa.org

- 101 Constitution Avenue N.W., Suite 705 East, Washington D.C. 20001
  Phone: (202) 742-4375; Fax: (202) 742-4377

Rock and Roll Hall of Fame and Museum

www.rockhall.com

- One Key Plaza, Cleveland, OH 44114
  Phone: (216) 781-7025

SESAC, Inc.*

www.sesac.com

- 55 Music Square East, Nashville, TN 37203
  Phone: (615) 320-0055; Fax: (615) 329-9627
- 152 West 57th Street, 57th Floor, New York, NY 10019
  Phone: (212) 586-3450; Fax: (212) 489-5699
- 501 Santa Monica Boulevard, Suite 450, Santa Monica, CA 90401-2430
  Phone: (310) 393-9671; Fax: (310) 393-6497

Songwriters Guild of America (SGA)

www.songwritersguild.com

- 1500 Harbor Boulevard, Weehawken, NJ 07086-6732
  Phone: (201) 867-7603; Fax: (201) 867-7535
- 6430 Sunset Boulevard, Suite 705, Hollywood, CA 90028
  Phone: (323) 462-1108; Fax: (323) 462-5430
- 209 Tenth Avenue South, Suite 534, Nashville TN 37203
  Phone: (615) 742-9945; Fax: (615) 742-9948
- 200 West 72nd Street, Suite 35, New York, NY 10036
  Phone: (917) 309-7869

U.S. Copyright Office

www.copyright.gov

- 101 Independence Avenue SE, Washington, DC 20559-6000
  Phone: (202) 707-9100

*Performing Rights Societies

RECOMMENDED READINGS

Brabec, Jeffrey, and Todd Brabec. *Music, Money, and Success: The Insider's Guide to Making Money in the Music Industry.* 4th ed. New York: Schirmer Trade Books, 2004.

Braheny, John. *The Craft and Business of Songwriting.* 2nd ed. Cincinnati: Writer's Digest Books, 2001.

Cahn, Sammy. *Sammy Cahn's Rhyming Dictionary.* New York: Cherry Lane Music, 2002.

Davis, Sheila. *The Craft of Lyric Writing.* Cincinnati: Writer's Digest Books, 1985.

Davis, Sheila. *Successful Lyric Writing: A Step-by-Step Course & Workbook.* Cincinnati: Writer's Digest Books, 1988.

Halloran, Mark, ed. *The Musician's Business and Legal Guide.* 3rd ed. Upper Saddle River, N.J.: Prentice Hall, 2001.

Jasen, David A. *Tin Pan Alley: The Composers, the Songs, the Performers, and Their Times: The Golden Age of American Popular Music from 1886 to 1956.* New York: D.I. Fine, 1988.

Kasha, Al, and Joel Hirschhorn. *If They Ask You, You Can Write a Song.* Updated ed. New York: Simon & Schuster, 1990.

Koller, Fred. *How to Pitch and Promote Your Songs.* 3rd. ed. New York: Allworth Press, 2001.

Monaco, Bob, and James Riordan. *The Platinum Rainbow: How to Succeed in the Music Business Without Selling Your Soul.* Newly rev. ed. Chicago: Contemporary Books, 1988.

Passman, Donald S. *All You Need to Know About the Music Business.* 5th ed. New York: Free Press, 2003.

Rapaport, Diane Sward. *How to Make & Sell Your Own Recording: The Complete Guide to Independent Recording.* Rev. 5th ed. Upper Saddle River, N.J.: Prentice Hall, 1999.

Siegel, Alan H. *Breakin' Into the Music Business.* 2nd ed. Port Chester, N.Y.: Cherry Lane Books, 1986.

Songwriter's Market. Cincinnati: Writer's Digest Books. Annual.

SAMPLE SGA CONTRACT

The Songwriters Guild of America

Note to songwriters: (A) Do not sign this contract if it has any changes unless you have first discussed such changes with the Guild; (B) For your protection please send a fully executed copy of this contract to the Guild.

POPULAR SONGWRITERS CONTRACT
©Copyright 1978 AGAC

AGREEMENT made this _____ day of _____, 20_____, between _____ (hereinafter called "Publisher") and _____ (Jointly and/or hereinafter collectively called "Writer");

WITNESSETH:

1. The Writer hereby assigns, transfers and delivers to the Publisher a certain heretofore unpublished original musical composition, written and/or composed by the above-named Writer now entitled _____ (hereinafter referred to as "the composition"), including the title, words and music thereof, and the right to secure copyright therein throughout the entire world, and to have and to hold the said copyright and all rights of whatsoever nature thereunder existing, for _____ years from the date of this contract or 35 years from the date of the first release of a commercial sound recording of the composition, whichever term ends earlier, unless this contract is sooner terminated in accordance with the provisions hereof.

2. In all respects this contract shall be subject to any existing agreements between the parties hereto and the following small performing rights licensing organization with which Writer and Publisher are affiliated: (ASCAP, BMI, SESAC). Nothing contained herein shall, or shall be deemed to, alter, vary or modify the rights of Writer and Publisher to share in, receive and retain the proceeds distributed to them by such small performing rights licensing organization pursuant to their respective agreement with it.

3. The Writer hereby warrants that the composition is his sole, exclusive and original work, that he has full right and power to make this contract, and that there exists no adverse claim to or in the composition, except as aforesaid in Paragraph 2 hereof and except such rights as are specifically set forth in paragraph 23 hereof.

4. In consideration of this contract, the Publisher agrees to pay the Writer as follows:

    (a) $_____ as an advance against royalties, receipt of which is hereby acknowledged, which sum shall remain the property of the Writer and shall be deductible only from payments hereafter becoming due the Writer under this contract.

    (b) In respect of regular piano copies sold and paid for in the United States and Canada, the following royalties per copy:
    _____% (in no case, however, less than 10%) of the wholesale selling price of the first 200,000 copies or less; plus
    _____% (in no case, however, less than 12%) of the wholesale selling price of copies in excess of 200,000 and not exceeding 500,000; plus
    _____% (in no case, however, less than 15%) of the wholesale selling price of copies in excess of 500,000.

    (c) _____% (in no case, however, less than 50%) of all net sums received by the Publisher in respect of regular piano copies, orchestrations, band arrangements, octavos, quartets, arrangements for combinations of voices and/or instruments, and/or other copies of the composition sold in any country other than the United States and Canada, provided, however, that if the Publisher should sell such copies through, or cause them to be sold by, a subsidiary or affiliate which is actually doing business in a foreign country, then in respect of such sales, the Publisher shall pay to the Writer not less than 5% of the marketed retail selling price in respect of each such copy sold and paid for.

    (d) In respect of each copy sold and paid for in the United States and Canada, or for export from the United States, of orchestrations, band arrangements, octavos, quartets, arrangements for combinations of voices and/or instruments, and/or other copies of the composition (other than regular piano copies) the following royalties on the wholesale selling price (after trade discounts, if any):
    _____% (in no case, however, less than 10%) on the first 200,000 copies or less; plus
    _____% (in no case, however, less than 12%) on all copies in excess of 200,000 and not exceeding 500,000; plus
    _____% (in no case, however, less than 15%) on all copies in excess of 500,000.

    (e) (i) If the composition, or any part thereof, is included in any song book, folio or similar publication issued by the Publisher containing at least four, but not more than twenty-five musical compositions, the royalty to be paid by the Publisher to the Writer shall be an amount determined by dividing 10% of the wholesale selling price (after trade discounts, if any) of the copies sold, among the total number of the Publisher's copyrighted musical compositions included in such publication. If such publication contains more than twenty-five musical compositions, the said 10% shall be increased by an additional .50% for each additional musical composition.

    (ii) If, pursuant to a license granted by the Publisher to a license not controlled by or affiliated with it, the composition, or any part thereof, is included in any song book, folio or similar publication, containing at least four musical compositions, the royalty to be paid by the Publisher to the Writer shall be that proportion of 50% of the gross amount received by it from the licensee, as the number of uses of the composition under the license and during the license period, bears to the total number of uses of the Publisher's copyrighted musical compositions under the license and during the license period.

 (iii) In computing the number of the Publisher's copyrighted musical compositions under subdivisions (i) and (ii) hereof, there shall be excluded musical compositions in the public domain and arrangements thereof and those with respect to which the Publisher does not currently publish and offer for sale regular piano copies.

 (iv) Royalties on publications containing less than four musical compositions shall be payable at regular piano copy rates.

(f) As to "professional material" not sold or resold, no royalty shall be payable. Free copies of the lyrics of the composition shall not be distributed except under the following conditions: (i) with the Writer's written consent; or (ii) when printed without music in limited numbers for charitable, religious or governmental purposes, or for similar public purposes, if no profit is derived, directly or indirectly; or (iii) when authorized for printing in a book, magazine or periodical, where such use is incidental to a novel or story (as distinguished from use in a book of lyrics or a lyric magazine or folio), provided that any such use shall bear the Writer's name and the proper copyright notice; or (iv) when distributed solely for the purpose of exploiting the composition, provided, that such exploitation is restricted to the distribution of limited numbers of such copies for the purpose of influencing the sale of the composition, that the distribution is independent of the sale of any other musical compositions, services, goods, wares or merchandise, and that no profit is made, directly or indirectly, in connection therewith.

(g) ____% (in no case, however, less than 50%) of:

All gross receipts of the Publisher in respect of any licenses (including statutory royalties) authorizing the manufacture of parts of instruments serving to mechanically reproduce the composition, or to use the composition in synchronization with sound motion pictures, or to reproduce it upon electrical transcription for broadcasting purposes; and of any and all gross receipts of the Publisher from any other source or right now known or which may hereafter come into existence, except as provided in Paragraph 2.

(h) If the Publisher administers licenses authorizing the manufacture of parts of instruments serving to mechanically reproduce said composition, or the use of said composition in synchronization or in timed relation with sound motion pictures or its reproduction upon electrical transcriptions, or any of them, through an agent, trustee or other administrator acting for a substantial part of the industry and not under the exclusive control of the Publisher (hereinafter sometimes referred to as licensing agent), the Publisher, in determining his receipts, shall be entitled to deduct from gross license fees paid by the Licensees, a sum equal to the charges paid by the Publisher to said licensing agent, provided, however, that in respect to synchronization or timed relation with sound motion pictures, said deduction shall in no event exceed $150.00 or 10% of said gross license fee, whichever is less; in connection with the manufacture of parts of instruments serving to mechanically reproduce said composition, said deduction shall not exceed 10% of said gross license fee.

(i) The Publisher agrees that the use of the composition will not be included in any bulk or block license heretofore or hereafter granted, and that it will not grant any bulk license to include the same, without the written consent of the Writer in each instance, except (i) that the Publisher may grant such licenses with respect to electrical transcription for broadcasting purposes, but in such event, the Publisher shall pay to the Writer that proportion of 50% of the gross amount received by it under each such license as the number of uses of the composition under each such license during each such license period bears to the total number of uses of the Publisher's copyrighted musical compositions under each such license during each such license period; in computing the number of the Publisher's copyrighted musical compositions for this purpose, there shall be excluded musical compositions in the public domain and arrangements thereof and those with respect to which the Publisher does not currently publish and offer for sale regular piano copies; (ii) that the Publisher may appoint agents or representatives in countries outside the United States and Canada to use and to grant licenses for the use of the composition on the customary royalty fee basis under which the Publisher shall receive not less than 10% of the marked retail selling price in respect of regular piano copies, and 50% of all other revenue; if, in connection with any such bulk of block license, the Publisher shall have received any advance, the Writer shall not be entitled to share therein, but no part of said advance shall be deducted in computing composition's earnings under said bulk or block license. A bulk or block license shall be deemed to mean any license or agreement, domestic or foreign, whereby rights are granted in respect of two or more musical compositions.

(j) Except to the extent that the Publisher and Writer have heretofore or may hereafter assign to or vest in the small performing rights licensing organization with which the Writer and Publisher are affiliated, the said rights or the right to grant licenses therefor, it is agreed that no licenses shall be granted without the written consent, in each instance, of the Writer for the use of the composition by means of television, or by any means, or for any purposes not commercially established, or for which licenses were not granted by the Publisher on musical compositions prior to June 1, 1937.

(k) The Publisher shall not, without the written consent of the Writer in each case, give or grant any right or license (i) to use the title of the composition, or (ii) for the exclusive use of the composition in any form or for any purpose, or for any period of time, or for any territory, other than its customary arrangements with foreign publishers, or (iii) to give a dramatic representation of the composition or to dramatize the plot or story thereof, or (iv) for a vocal rendition of the composition in synchronization with sound motion pictures, or (v) for any synchronization use thereof, or (vi) for the use of the composition or a quotation or excerpt therefrom in any article, book, periodical, advertisement or other similar publication. If, however, the Publisher shall give to the Writer written notice by certified mail, return receipt requested, or telegram, specifying the right or license to be given or granted, the name of the licensee and the terms and conditions thereof, including the price or other compensation to be received therefor, then, unless the Writer (or any one or more of them) shall, within five business days after the delivery of such notice to the address of the Writer hereinafter designated, object thereto, the Publisher may grant such right or license in accordance with the said notice without first obtaining the consent of the Writer. Such notice shall be deemed sufficient if sent to the Writer at the address or addresses hereinafter designated or at the address or addresses last furnished to the Publisher in writing by the Writer.

(l) Any portion of the receipts which may become due to the Writer from license fees (in excess of offsets), whether received directly from the licensee or from any licensing agent of the Publisher, shall, if not paid immediately on the receipt thereof by the Publisher, belong to the Writer and shall be held in trust for the Writer until payment is made; the ownership of said trust fund by the Writer shall not be questioned whether the monies are physically segregated or not.

(m) The Publisher agrees that it will not issue any license as a result of which it will receive any financial benefit in which the Writer does not participate.

(n) On all regular piano copies, orchestrations, band or other arrangements, octavos, quartets, commercial sound recordings and other reproductions of the composition or parts thereof, in whatever form and however produced, Publisher shall include or cause to be included, in addition to the copyright notice, the name of the Writer, and Publisher shall include a similar requirement in every license or authorization issued by it with respect to the composition.

5. Whenever the term "Writer" is used herein, it shall be deemed to mean all of the persons herein defined as "Writer" and any and all royalties herein provided to be paid to the Writer shall be paid equally to such persons if there be more than one, unless otherwise provided in Paragraph 23.

6. (a) (i) The Publisher shall, within ____ months from the date of this contract (the "initial period"), cause a commercial sound recording of the composition to be made and released in the customary form and through the customary commercial channels. If at the end of such initial period a sound recording has not been made and released, as above provided, then, subject to the provisions of the next succeeding subdivision, this contract shall terminate.

(ii) If, prior to the expiration of the initial period, Publisher pays the Writer the sum of $_____ (which shall not be charged against or recoupable out of any advances, royalties or other monies theretofore paid, then due, or which thereafter may become due the Writer from the Publisher pursuant to this contract or otherwise), Publisher shall have an additional ____ months (the "additional period") commencing with the end of the initial period, within which to cause such commercial sound recording to be made and released as provided in subdivision (i) above. If at the end of the additional period a commercial recording has not been made and released, as above provided, then this contract shall terminate.

(iii) Upon termination pursuant to this Paragraph 6(a), all rights of any and every nature in and to the composition and in and to any and all copyrights secured thereon in the United States and throughout the world shall automatically re-vest in and become the property of the Writer and shall be reassigned to him by the Publisher. The Writer shall not be obligated to return or pay to the Publisher any advance or indebtedness as a condition of such re-assignment; the said re-assignment shall be in accordance with and subject to the provisions of Paragraph 8 hereof, and, in addition, the Publisher shall pay to the Writer all gross sums which it has theretofore or may thereafter receive of the composition.

(b) The Publisher shall furnish, or cause to be furnished, to the Writer six copies of the commercial sound recording referred to in Paragraph 6(a).

(c) The Publisher shall [Select (i) or (ii)] __(i) within 30 days after the initial release of a commercial recording of the composition, make, publish and offer for sale regular piano copies of the composition in the form and through the channels customarily employed by it for that purpose; __(ii) within 30 days after execution of this contract make a piano arrangement or lead sheet of the composition and furnish six copies thereof to the Writer.

In the event neither subdivision (i) nor (ii) of this paragraph (c) is selected, the provisions of subdivision (ii) shall be automatically deemed to have been selected by the parties.

7. (a) Each copyright on the composition in countries other than the United States shall be secured only in the name of the Publisher, and the Publisher shall not at any time divest itself of said foreign copyright directly or indirectly.

(b) No rights shall be granted by the Publisher in the composition to any foreign publisher or licensee inconsistent with the terms hereof, nor shall any foreign publication rights in the composition be given to a foreign publisher or licensee unless and until the Publisher shall have complied with the provisions of Paragraph 6 hereof.

(c) If foreign rights in the composition are separately conveyed, otherwise than as a part of the Publisher's current and/or future catalog, not less than 50% of any advance received in respect thereof shall be credited to the account of and paid to the Writer.

(d) The percentage of the Writer on monies received from foreign sources shall be computed on the Publisher's net receipts, provided, however, that no deductions shall be made for offsets of monies due from the Publisher to said foreign sources; or for advances made by such foreign sources to the Publisher, unless the Writer shall have received at least 50% of said advances.

(e) In computing the receipts of the Publisher from licenses granted in respect of synchronization with sound motion pictures, or in respect of any world-wide licenses, or in respect of licenses granted by the Publisher for use of the composition in countries other than the United States, no amount shall be deducted for payments or allocations to publishers or licenses in such countries.

8. Upon the termination or expiration of this contract, all rights of any and every nature in and to the composition and in and to any and all copyrights secured thereon in the United States and throughout the world, shall re-vest in and become the property of the Writer, and shall be re-assigned to the Writer by the Publisher free of any and all encumbrances of any nature whatsoever, provided that:

    (a) If the Publisher, prior to such termination or expiration, shall have granted a domestic license for the use of the composition, not inconsistent with the terms and provisions of this contract, the re-assignment may be subject to the terms of such license.

    (b) Publisher shall assign to the Writer all rights which it may have under any such agreement or license referred to in subdivision (a) in respect of the composition, including, but not limited to, the right to receive all royalties or other monies earned by the composition thereunder after the date of termination or expiration of this contract. Should the Publisher thereafter receive or be credited with any royalties or other monies so earned, it shall pay the same to the Writer.

    (c) The Writer shall not be obligated to return or pay to the Publisher any advance or indebtedness as a condition of the reassignment provided for in this Paragraph 8, and shall be entitled to receive the plates and copies of the composition in the possession of the Publisher.

    (d) Publisher shall pay any and all royalties which may have accrued to the Writer prior to such termination or expiration.

    (e) The Publisher shall execute any and all documents and do any and all acts or things necessary to effect any and all reassignments to the Writer herein provided for.

9. If the Publisher desires to exercise a right in and to the composition now known or which may hereafter become known, but for which no specific provision has been made herein, the Publisher shall give written notice to the Writer thereof. Negotiations respecting all the terms and conditions of any such disposition shall thereupon be entered into between the Publisher and the Writer and no such right shall be exercised until specific agreement has been made.

10. The Publisher shall render to the Writer, hereafter, royalty statements accompanied by remittance of the amount due at the times such statements and remittances shall be rendered either semi-annually or quarterly and not more than forty-five days after the end of such semi-annual or quarterly period, as the case may be. The Writer may at any time, or from time to time, make written request for a detailed royalty statement, and the Publisher shall, within sixty days, comply therewith. Such royalty statements shall set forth in detail various items, foreign and domestic, for which royalties are payable thereunder and the amounts thereof, including, but not limited to, the number of copies sold and the number of uses made in each royalty category. If a use is made in a publication of the character provided in Paragraph 4, subdivision (e) hereof, there shall be included in said royalty statement the title of said publication, the publisher or issuer thereof, the date of and number of uses, the gross license fee received in connection with each publication, the share thereto of all the writers under contract with the Publisher, and the Writer's share thereof. There shall likewise be included in said statement a description of every other use of the composition, and if by a licensee or licensees their names, and if said use is upon a part of an instrument serving to reproduce the composition mechanically, the type of mechanical reproduction, the title of the label thereon, the name or names of the artists performing the same, together with the gross license fees received, and the Writer's share thereof.

11. (a) The Publisher shall from time to time, upon written demand of the Writer or his representative, permit the Writer or his representative to inspect at the place of business of the Publisher, all books, records and documents relating to the composition and all licenses granted, uses had and payments made therefor, such right of inspection to include, but not by way of limitation, the right to examine all original accountings and records relating to uses and payments by manufacturers of commercial sound recordings and music rolls; and the Writer or his representative may appoint an accountant who shall at any time during usual business hours have access to all records of the Publisher relating to the composition for the purpose of verifying royalty statements rendered or which are delinquent under the terms hereof.

    (b) The Publisher shall, upon written demand of the Writer or his representative, cause any licensing agent in the United States and Canada to furnish to the Writer or his representative, statements showing in detail all licenses granted, uses had and payments made in connection with the composition, which licenses or permits were granted, or payments were received, by or through said licensing agent, and to permit the Writer or his representative to inspect at the place of business of such licensing agent, all books, records and documents of such licensing agent, relating thereto. Any and all agreements made by the Publisher with any such licensing agent shall provide that any such licensing agent will comply with the terms and provisions hereof. In the event that the Publisher shall instruct such licensing agent to furnish to the Writer or his representative statements as provided for herein, and to permit the inspection of the books, records and documents as herein provided, then if such licensing agent should refuse to comply with the said instructions, or any of them, the Publisher agrees to institute and prosecute diligently and in good faith such action or proceedings as may be necessary to compel compliance with the said instructions.

    (c) With respect to foreign licensing agents, the Publisher shall make available the books or records of said licensing agents in countries outside of the United States and Canada to the extent such books or records are available to the Publisher, except that the Publisher may in lieu thereof make available any accountants' reports and audits which the Publisher is able to obtain.

    (d) If as a result of any examination of books, records or documents pursuant to Paragraphs 11(a), 11(b) or 11(c) hereof, it is determined that, with respect to any royalty statement rendered by or on behalf of the Publisher to the Writer, the Writer is owed a sum equal to or greater than five percent of the sum shown on that royalty statement as being due to the Writer, then the Publisher shall pay to the Writer the entire cost of such examination, not to exceed 50% of the amount shown to be due the Writer.

(e) (i) In the event the Publisher administers its own licenses for the manufacture of parts of instruments serving to mechanically reproduce the composition rather than employing a licensing agent for that purpose, the Publisher shall include in each license agreement a provision permitting the Publisher, the Writer or their respective representatives to inspect, at the place of business of such licensee, all books, records and documents of such licensee relating to such license. Within 30 days after written demand by the Writer, the Publisher shall commence to inspect such licensee's books, records and documents and shall furnish a written report of such inspection to the Writer within 90 days following such demand. If the Publisher fails, after written demand by the Writer, to so inspect the licensee's books, records and documents, or fails to furnish such report, the Writer or his representative may inspect such licensee's books, records and documents at his own expense.

(ii) In the further event that the Publisher and the licensee referred to in subdivision (i) above are subsidiaries or affiliates of the same entity or one is a subsidiary or affiliate of the other, then, unless the Publisher employs a licensing agent to administer the licenses referred to in subdivision (i) above, the Writer shall have the right to make the inspection referred to in subdivision (i) above without the necessity of making written demand on the Publisher as provided in subdivision (i) above.

(iii) If as a result of any inspection by the Writer pursuant to subdivisions (i) and (ii) of this subparagraph (e) the Writer recovers additional monies from the licensee, the Publisher and the Writer shall share equally in the cost of such inspection.

12. If the Publisher shall fail or refuse, within sixty days after written demand, to furnish or cause to be furnished, such statements, books, records or documents, or to permit inspection thereof, as provided for in Paragraphs 10 and 11 hereof, or within thirty days after written demand, to make the payment of any royalties due under this contract, then the Writer shall be entitled, upon ten days written notice, to terminate this contract. However if the Publisher shall:

(a) Within the said ten-day period serve upon the Writer a written notice demanding arbitration; and

(b) Submit to arbitration its claim that it has complied with its obligation to furnish statements, books, records or documents, or permitted inspection thereof or to pay royalties, as the case may be, or both, and thereafter comply with any award of the arbitrator within ten days after such award or within such time as the arbitrator may specify; then this contract shall continue in full force and effect as if the Writer had not sent such notice of termination. If the Publisher shall fail to comply with the foregoing provisions, then this contract shall be deemed to have been terminated as of the date of the Writer's written notice of termination.

13. No derivative work prepared under authority of Publisher during the term of this contract may be utilized by Publisher or any other party after termination or expiration of this contract.

14. All written demands and notices provided for herein shall be sent by certified mail, return receipt requested.

15. Any legal action brought by the Publisher against any alleged infringer of the composition shall be initiated and prosecuted at its sole cost and expense, but if the Publisher should fail, within thirty days after written demand, to institute such action, the Writer shall be entitled to institute such suit at his cost and expense. All sums recovered as a result of any such action shall, after the deduction of the reasonable expense thereof, be divided equally between the Publisher and the Writer. No settlement of any such action may be made by either party without first notifying the other; in the event that either party should object to such settlement, then such settlement shall not be made if the party objecting assumes the prosecution of the action and all expenses thereof, except that any sums thereafter recovered shall be divided equally between the Publisher and the Writer after the deduction of the reasonable expenses thereof.

16. (a) If a claim is presented against the Publisher alleging that the composition is an infringement upon some other work or a violation of any other right of another, and because thereof the Publisher is jeopardized, it shall forthwith serve a written notice upon the Writer setting forth the full details of such claim. The pendency of said claim shall not relieve the Publisher of the obligation to make payment of the royalties to the Writer hereunder, unless the Publisher shall deposit said royalties as and when they would otherwise be payable, in an account in the joint names of the Publisher and the Writer in a bank or trust company in New York, New York, if the Writer on the date of execution of this contract resides East of the Mississippi River, or in Los Angeles, California, if the Writer on the date of execution of this contract resides West of the Mississippi River. If no suit be filed within nine months after said written notice from the Publisher to the Writer, all monies deposited in said joint account shall be paid over to the Writer plus any interest which may have been earned thereon.

(b) Should an action be instituted against the Publisher claiming that the composition its an infringement upon some other work or a violation of any right of another, the Publisher shall forthwith serve written notice upon the Writer containing the full details of such claim. Notwithstanding the commencement of such action, the Publisher shall continue to pay the royalties hereunder to the Writer unless it shall, from and after the date of the service of the summons, deposit said royalties as and when they would otherwise be payable, in an account in the joint names of the Publisher and the Writer in a bank or trust company in New York, New York, if the Writer on the date of execution of this contract resides East of the Mississippi River, or in Los Angeles, California, if the Writer on the date of execution of this contract resides West of the Mississippi River. If the said suit shall be finally adjudicated in favor of the Publisher or shall be settled, there shall be released and paid to the Writer all of such sums held in escrow less any amount paid out of the Writer's share with the Writer's written consent in settlement of said action. Should the said suit finally result adversely to the Publisher, the said amount on the deposit shall be released to the Publisher to the extent or damage it incurs and the balance shall be paid over to the Writer.

(c) In any of the foregoing events, however, the Writer shall be entitled to payment of said royalties or the money so deposited at and after such time as he files with the Publisher a surety company bond, or a bond in other form acceptable to the Publisher, in the sum of such payments to secure the return thereof to the extent that the Publisher may be entitled to such return. The foregoing payments or deposits or the filing of a bond shall be without prejudice to the rights of the Publisher or Writer in the premises.

17. Any and all differences, disputes or controversies arising out of or in connection with this contract shall be submitted to arbitration before a sole arbitrator under the then prevailing rules of the American Arbitration Association. The location of the arbitration shall be New York, New York, if the Writer on the date of execution of this contract resides East of the Mississippi River, or in Los Angeles, California, if the Writer on the date of execution of this contract resides West of the Mississippi River. The parties hereby individually and jointly agree to abide by and perform any award rendered in such arbitration. Judgment upon any such award rendered may be entered in any court having jurisdiction thereof.

18. Except to the extent herein otherwise expressly provided, the Publisher shall not sell, transfer, assign, convey, encumber or otherwise dispose of the composition or the copyright or copyrights secured thereon without the prior written consent of the Writer. The Writer has been induced to enter into this contract in reliance upon the value to him of the personal service and ability of the Publisher in the exploitation of the composition, and by reason thereof it is the intention of the parties and the essence of the relationship between them that the rights herein granted to the Publisher shall remain with the Publisher and that the same shall not pass to any other person, including, without limitations, successors to or receivers or trustees of the property of the Publisher, either by act or deed of the Publisher or by operation of law, and in the event of the voluntary or involuntary bankruptcy of the Publisher, this contract shall terminate, provided, however, that the composition may be included by the Publisher in a bona fide voluntary sale of its music business or its entire catalog of musical compositions, or in a merger or consolidation of the Publisher with a another corporation, in which event the Publisher shall immediately give written notice thereof to the Writer; and provided further that the composition and the copyright therein may be assigned by the Publisher to a subsidiary or affiliated company generally engaged in the music publishing business. Any such transfer or assignment shall, however, be conditioned upon the execution and delivery by the transferee or assignee to the Writer of an agreement to be bound by and to perform all of the terms and conditions of this contract to be performed on the part of the Publisher.

19. A subsidiary, affiliate, or any person, firm or corporation controlled by the Publisher or by such subsidiary or affiliate, as used in this contract, shall be deemed to include any person, firm or corporation, under common control with, or the majority of whose stock or capital contribution is owned or controlled by the Publisher or by any of its officers, directors, partners or associates, or whose policies and actions are subject to domination or control by the Publisher or any of its officers, directors, partners or associates.

20. The amounts and percentages specified in this contract shall be deemed to be the amounts and percentages agreed upon by the parties hereto, unless other amounts or percentages are inserted in the blank spaces provided therefor.

21. This contract is binding upon and shall inure to the benefit of the parties hereto and their respective successors in interest (as hereinbefore limited). If the Writer (or one or more of them) shall not be living, any notices may be given to, or consents given by, his or their successors in interest. No change or modification of this contract shall be effective unless reduced to writing and signed by the parties hereto. The words in this contract shall be so construed that the singular shall include the plural and the plural shall include the singular where the context so requires and the masculine shall include the feminine and the feminine shall include the masculine where the context so requires.

22. The paragraph headings are inserted only as a matter of convenience and for reference, and in no way define, limit or describe the scope or intent of this contract nor in any way affect this contract.

23. [Special Provisions]

Publisher: _____ Writer: _____

By: _____ Address: _____

Address: _____ Soc. Sec.#: _____

Witness: _____ Witness: _____

EXPLANATION OF SGA CONTRACT

SGA CONTRACT | The Songwriters Guild of America is a voluntary association of songwriters; it is not a union. The SGA Contract is thus not a negotiated contract between publishers and the SGA. Rather, the Contract has been prepared by SGA and its legal counsel and represents what SGA believes to be the best minimum songwriter contract available.

The Contract is an agreement between a songwriter (or co-writers) and a publisher. It sets forth the rights and obligations of both parties, with respect to a song or songs.

In order to facilitate a general understanding of the terms of the Contract, the following is a brief summary of its highlights.

PARAGRAPH 1 | Here, the songwriter assigns his song to a publisher, for use throughout the world, for a designated number of years. The period of use should not exceed 40 years, or 35 years from the date of the first release of a commercial sound recording (the term reflects the provisions of the 1976 Copyright Revision Law). The shorter the term, the better for the songwriter, because if the song is successful, the songwriter can renegotiate more favorable financial terms at an earlier time. The length of the term will often depend on the bargaining strength and reputation of the songwriter.

PARAGRAPH 2 | This recognizes that the songwriter is a member of a particular performing rights society (either ASCAP, BMI or SESAC) and that this Contract will not interfere with the songwriter's collection of performing rights proceeds directly from his/her performing rights society. It is crucial that the songwriter and publisher are members of the same performing rights society.

PARAGRAPH 3 | Here, the songwriter warrants that the song is her or her own original creation and, as such, the songwriter has the right to enter into the agreement.

PARAGRAPH 4 | The paragraph sets forth royalties to be paid for various types of uses of the song. Note that the Contract sets forth minimum amounts that the songwriter must receive. Of course, the songwriter is free to attempt to negotiate for higher royalty rates. If no amounts are filled in, the minimum amounts apply. Paragraph 4(k) provides that the initial publisher may not, without the songwriter's written consent, grant certain licenses not specifically permitted by the Contract (e.g. use of the title of the song; to give a dramatic representation of the song; synchronization, licenses, etc.).

PARAGRAPH 5 | This paragraph applies if the song or songs being sold were written by more than one songwriter. If so, each songwriter will share royalties equally, unless specified otherwise in Paragraph 23.

PARAGRAPH 6 | This paragraph requires the publisher to have a commercial sound recording of the song made and released within 12 months from the date of the Contract or to pay the songwriter a sum of not less than $250.00 dollars for the right to extend this period for not more than six months. If the publisher does not comply, the Contract terminates and all rights return to the songwriter. This paragraph also provides that the publisher provide the songwriter with six copies of the sound recording once it is cut. Also, under paragraph 6(c), it states that the publisher must either (i) publish, and offer for sale, regular piano copies of the song within thirty days of release of the sound recording; or, (ii) make a piano arrangement or lead sheet of the song within thirty days of execution of the Contract—with six copies to be given to the songwriter. Both parties must select which of the two alternatives will apply.

PARAGRAPH 7 | This paragraph deals with the publisher's sub-licensing of the song in foreign countries. It guarantees that the songwriter will receive no less than 50% of the revenue by the publisher from rights licensed outside the U.S.

PARAGRAPH 8 | This section explains what happens when the Contract terminates (that is, all rights revert to the songwriter, subject to any outstanding licenses issued by the publisher and the latter's duty to account for monies received after termination).

PARAGRAPH 9 | This deals with exploitation of the song in a manner not yet contemplated and, thus, not specifically covered in the Contract. Any such exploitation must be mutually agreed upon by the songwriter and the publisher.

PARAGRAPHS 10, 11 AND 12 | These paragraphs deal with the method of payment of royalties to the songwriter and the songwriter's right to inspect the publisher's books.

PARAGRAPH 13 | Various uses of the song, such as sound recordings and arrangements, are considered derivative works under the Copyright Law. Often, such derivative works can have more financial value than the original sheet music. This provision provides that when the Contract terminates, the publisher loses all rights in such derivative works, as well as in the original version of the song.

PARAGRAPHS 15 AND 16 | These paragraphs deal with bringing lawsuits against those who infringe upon the songwriter's rights and defending lawsuits in the event someone claims that the song infringed upon a copyright.

PARAGRAPH 17 | In the event there is a dispute between the songwriter and the publisher that they cannot resolve, such dispute is to be settled by arbitration (generally considered a more expeditious and inexpensive means of settling claims)."

PARAGRAPH 18 | This places restrictions on a publisher's rights to sell the songwriter's song to another publisher-other than as part of the publisher's entire catalog.

INDEX

More Great Ideas
From Writer's Digest Books!

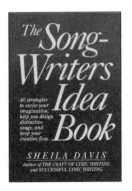

The Songwriter's Idea Book by Sheila Davis. This critically acclaimed reference for aspiring and professional songwriters offers practical exercises and effective strategies to help you through all stages of the lyric writing process. Examples from 100 country, pop, theater, and cabaret lyrics will help you to understand the relationship between personality type, brain function, and your writing style.
ISBN 0-89879-519-2, paperback, 240 pages, #10320

Songwriter's Market edited by Ian Bessler. Musicians and songwriters rely on this annually updated guide to provide them with contact information and submission procedures for record companies, booking agents, music producers and others instrumental in establishing a successful music career. This year's edition contains more than 1,000 updated listings, informative interviews, and networking resources.
ISBN 1-58297-398-9, paperback, 472 pages, #11022

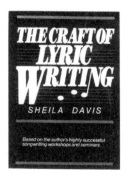

The Craft of Lyric Writing by Sheila Davis. Successful author and songwriter Sheila Davis provides answers to hundreds of fundamental songwriting questions in this best-selling how-to guide for aspiring lyricists. Learn to write professional, appealing music that will catch the attention of industry pros and help you begin a successful music career.
ISBN 0-89879-149-9, hardcover, 350 pages, #01148

**These and other fine books from Writer's Digest Books
are available at your local bookstore or online supplier.**